The

Year

of the

Poet V

October 2018

The Poetry Posse

inner child press, ltd.

The Poetry Posse 2018

Gail Weston Shazor

Shareef Abdur Rasheed

Teresa E. Gallion

hülya n. yılmaz

Kimberly Burnham

Tzemin Ition Tsai

Elizabeth Esguerra Castillo

Jackie Davis Allen

Nizar Sartawi

Caroline 'Ceri' Nazareno

Ashok K. Bhargava

Alicja Maria Kuberska

Swapna Behera

William S. Peters, Sr.

General Information

The Year of the Poet V
October 2018 Edition
Series # 58

The Poetry Posse

1st Edition : 2018

Publisher Information
1st Edition : Inner Child Press
intouch@innerchildpress.com
www.innerchildpress.com

ISBN-13 : 978-1-970020-64-9 (inner child press, ltd.)

$ 12.99

WHAT WOULD **LIFE** BE WITHOUT A LITTLE **POETRY?**

$\mathcal{D}$edication

This Book is dedicated to

Poetry . . .

The Poetry Posse

past, present & future

our Patrons and Readers

the Spirit of our Everlasting Muse

&

the Power of the Pen

to effectuate change!

In the darkness of my life
I heard the music
I danced . . .
and the Light appeared
and I dance

Janet P. Caldwell

Janet Perkins Caldwell

Rest In Peace

February 14, 1959 ~ September 20, 2016

Rest In Peace Dear Brother

Alan W. Jankowski

16 March 1961 ~ 10 March 2017

Poets . . .
sowing seeds in the
Conscious Garden of Life,
that those who have yet to come
may enjoy the Flowers.

Table of Contents

The Poetry Posse

Table of Contents . . . *continued*

October Featured Poets   99

$\mathcal{F}$oreword

Let's talk bengali people, yotp oct. 2018

Our monthly publication Year of the Poet nearing completion of 5 years in print has this year 2018 a theme featuring the peoples that comprise the inhabitants of planet earth. The maker of both has created this planet our home and created mankind/human beings to inhabit it. He made mankind into tribes and nations that they may know one another (Identity, variety) not despise each other because the best of you are the most devoted, god fearing amongst you (Qur'an:49,13). This month we take a look at the Bengali People, the third largest ethnic group in the world after the Han Chinese and Arabs.

Bengalis are an Indo-Aryan people native to the region of Bengal in south Asia which is presently divided between Bangladesh and the Indian states of West Bengal, Tripura, Assam. They speak the Bengali language, one of the most easterly representatives of the Indo-European language family. They have a very detailed history that spans many centuries. Here for we will try to briefly explore some of the notable milestones.

The Bengali people are of a diverse origin through the merging of various communities that migrated into the region over many centuries. the earliest inhabitants are said to had been the Vedda from Sri Lanka formally Ceylon. Later came Mediterranean peoples who spoke Indo-European languages. In the 8th century Arabs, Turks, and Persians came to the region. In time these various groups merged to become the Bengali People. The name Bengali/Bangali is said to derive from the word " Bang " from the tribe Bang or Banga that settled in the region around 1000BCE.

Most of the Bengali people today in Bangladesh are Sunni Muslims, more than 90 per cent while in West Bengal the majority are Hindu. Islam came to the region in the 13th century. At the time the population was comprised of Hindus and Buddhists. Following the arrival of Muslims most of the residents eventually embraced Islam. In the western region Hinduism was predominant.

Besides Bengali Muslims, Bengali Hindus and Bengali Buddhists Bengali Christians are also included in the major religious groups. Counted in the minority are Bengali Jews, Bengali Sikhs and Bengali Baha'is

In the 21st century most of the Bengali population live in rural areas in both Bangladesh and West Bengal. Many are farmers, the main crops being rice and jute but including legumes and oil seeds. Mostly men tend to the farming and the women manage domestic affairs. It's a different matter in the cities where men and women pursue careers in professions such as medicine and education.

The Mughal Empire conquered Bengal in the 16th century including Dhaka during the time of Emperor Akbar. A few Rajput tribes from his army permanently settled around Dhaka and surrounding lands. Later, in the early 17th century Islam Khan conquered all of Bengal. However, administration by governors appointed by the court of the Mughal Empire gave way to semi-independence of the area under the Nawabs of Murshidabad, who nominally respected the sovereignty of the Mughals in Delhi.

The Bengal Subah province in the Mughal Empire was the wealthiest state in the subcontinent. Bengal's trade and wealth impressed the Mughals so much that it was described as the Paradise of the Nations by the Mughal Emperors.

Under Mughal rule, Bengal was a center of the worldwide muslin, silk and pearl trades. During the Mughal era, the most important center of cotton production was Bengal, particularly around its capital city of Dhaka, leading to muslin being called "daka" in distant markets such as Central Asia. Domestically, much of India depended on Bengali products such as rice, silks and cotton textiles. Overseas, Europeans depended on Bengali products such as cotton textiles, silks and opium; Bengal accounted for 40% of Dutch imports from Asia, for example, including more than 50% of textiles and around 80% of silks. From Bengal, saltpeter was also shipped to Europe, opium was sold in Indonesia, raw silk was exported to Japan and the Netherlands, cotton and silk textiles were exported to Europe, Indonesia, and Japan, cotton cloth was exported to the Americas and the Indian Ocean. Bengal also had a large shipbuilding industry. In terms of shipbuilding tonnage during the 16th–18th centuries, the annual output of Bengal alone totaled around 2,232,500 tons, larger than the combined output of the Dutch (450,000–550,000 tons), the British (340,000 tons), and North America (23,061 tons).

British colonization followed in the mid 17 hundred. After a series of Rebellions including the Indian independence movement in which Bengalis played a major role in India's independence from British ruled India through independent states created after the Lahore Resolution in 1943. There was a breakdown in Hindu-Muslim unity and the Muslim league adopted the Lahore Resolution and that lead to Partition from British India based on the Radcliffe Line in 1947.Later when Pakistan was formed there was a movement among Bengali Nationalist to succeed from Pakistan in the east which lead to the Bangladesh Liberation War against the Pakistani military junta in which 3 million died. Dec.16 1971 Dhaka was liberated after the intervention of the Indian Armed Forces leading to Pakistan's surrender and the birth of Bangladesh.

Regardless Hindu, Muslim etc. it is a part of Bengali culture to embrace various genres of Art that includes Music (baul and marfati). Film internationally acclaimed out of West Bengal many with a musical component.

Islamic art/architecture especially in Bangladesh prominent in many mosques, mausoleums, forts and gateways that survived the Mughal period. Bengali literature going back to before the 12th century. The Caitanya movement a deeply intense form of Hinduism inspired by a Hindu saint Caitanya (1485-1533) gave birth the development of Bengal poetry until the early 19th century when Western influence sparked a broad creative force. Stand out artists such as Nobel-Prize winning poet Rabindranath Tagore came out of that period.

This was just a small taste of historical information about the Bengali peoples, a human mosaic rich in diversity that today number over 300 million in a globally spread out diaspora including Pakistan, The United States, United Kingdom, Canada, the Middle east, Japan, South Korea, Malaysia, Singapore and Italy. Hopefully you found it informative. Peace/love/Blessings.

Shareef Abdur-Rasheed

AKA Zakir Flo
Poet, Author
Inner Child Press family member
Member of the Poetry Posse since Jan.2014

Poets, Writers . . . know that we are the enchanting magicians that nourishes the seeds of dreams and thoughts . . . it is our words that entice the hearts and minds of others to believe there is something grand about the possibilities that life has to offer and our words tease it forth into action . . . for you are the Poet, the Writer to whom the Gift of Words has been entrusted . . .

~ wsp

$\mathcal{P}$reface

Dear Family and Friends,

Yes I am excited? Once again, this is an understatement! As we are hitting another milestone, the 10th month of our fifth year of publication . . . I am elated. Our initial vision was to just perform at this level for the year of 2014. Since that time we have had the blessed opportunity to include many other wonderful word artists and storytellers in the Poetry Posse from lands, cultures and persuasions all over the world. We have featured hundreds of additional poets, thereby introducing their poetic offerings to our vast global readership.

In keeping with our effort and vision to expand the awareness of poets from all walks by making this offerings accessible, we at Inner Child Press will continue to make every volume a FREE Download. The books are also available for purchase at the affordable cost of $7.00 per volume.

In the previous years, our monthly themes were Flowers, Birds, Gemstones and Trees. This year we have elected to take a different direction by theming our offerings after *Cultures* of past and present. In each month's volume you will have the opportunity to not only read at least one poem themed by our Poetry Posse members about such culture, but we have included a few words about the culture in our prologue. The reasoning behind this is that now our poetry has the opportunity to be educational for not only the reader, but we poets as well. We hope you find the poetic offerings insightful as we use our poetic form to relay to you what we too have learned through our research in making our offering available to you, our readership.

In closing, we would like to thank you for being an integral part of our amazing journey.

Enjoy our amazing featured poets . . . they are amazing!

Building Cultural Bridges of understanding . . .

Bless Up

From our house to yours

Bill
The Poetry Posse
Inner Child Press

PS

Do Not forget about the World Healing, World Peace Poetry effort.

Available here

www.worldhealingworldpeacepoetry.com

or

Janet . . . gone too soon.

http://www.innerchildpress.com/janet-p-caldwell.php

For Free Downloads of Previous Issues of The Year of the Poet

www.innerchildpress.com/the-year-of-the-poet

poetry is . . .

Bengali

The Bengali culture encompasses the region in South Asia, which includes Bangladesh and the Indian states of West Bengal, Tripura and Assam (Barak Valley), where the Bengali language is the official and primary language. Bengal has a recorded history of over 1,400 years. The Bengali people are its dominant ethnolinguistic Tribe. The region has been a historical melting point, blending indigenous traditions with cosmopolitan influences from pan-Indian subcontinental empires. Bengal was the richest part of Medieval India and hosted the subcontinent's most advanced political and cultural centers during the British Raj.

For more information visit :
https://en.wikipedia.org/wiki/Culture_of_Bengal

The
Year
of the
Poet V

October 2018

The Poetry Posse

Poetry succeeds where instruction fails.

~ wsp

Gail
Weston
Shazor

This is a creative promise ~ my pen will speak to and for the world. Enamored with letters and respectful of their power, I have been writing for most of my life. A mother, daughter, sister and grandmother I give what I have been given, greatfilledly.

Author of . . .

"An Overstanding of an Imperfect Love"
&
Notes from the Blue Roof

Lies My Grandfathers Told Me

available at Inner Child Press.

www.facebook.com/gailwestonshazor
www.innerchildpress.com/gail-weston-shazor
navypoet1@gmail.com

I Close My Eyes

I close my eyes
And on the tip of my tongue
Taste the length of your neck
From the edge of beard
To your strong collarbone
The gold chain is simply
The ribbon on my package
Pecs ease into a flat belly
And gives way to my waist
Or at least the place
Where I love to kiss
The mmmm's escape
My parted lips with a sigh
When I touch the corner
Of your mouth
Down turned
Even when you smile
With full lips
Whispering a tune
Be it gospel or soul
Hearing the colors of life
In a deep timbre
You make me content
I am with you and
I am safe and
I close my eyes

Overstanding

Today I dreamed of the sun
With eyes wide open and looking
Through a window newly clean
Rag in one hand and windex in the other
And just for a moment I could
Smell the ocean wafting
A warm breeze across my feet
So I had to remove my socks
To see if I could wiggle my toes
In a sandy delight of pleasure
I can taste the greenness of
Of your heart holding onto mine
The windowpane seems a doorway
Only I have been asked to enter
When I listen, I can hear your voice
Folding the wings of brown pelicans
And whispering past the lushness
Of the bougainvillea vine
Sweet and sensuous lyrics
Sounding off tamarind clusters
And shooting carambola stars
Calling me to you throughout the day
Upon my prayers gazing beyond glass
I know that you are my overstanding

Alicja
Maria
Kuberska

.

Alicja Maria Kuberska – awarded Polish poetess, novelist, journalist, editor. She was born in 1960, in Świebodzin, Poland. She now lives in Inowrocław, Poland.

In 2011 she published her first volume of poems entitled: "The Glass Reality". Her second volume "Analysis of Feelings", was published in 2012. The third collection "Moments" was published in English in 2014, both in Poland and in the USA. In 2014, she also published the novel - "Virtual roses" and volume of poems "On the border of dream". Next year her volume entitled "Girl in the Mirror" was published in the UK and "Love me" , " (Not)my poem" in the USA. In 2015 she also edited anthology entitled "The Other Side of the Screen".

In 2016 she edited two volumes: "Taste of Love" (USA), "Thief of Dreams" (Poland) and international anthology entitled " Love is like Air" (USA). In 2017 she published volume entitled "View from the window" (Poland). She also edits series of anthologies entitled "Metaphor of Contemporary" (Poland)

Her poems have been published in numerous anthologies and magazines in Poland, the USA, the UK, Albania, Belgium, Chile, Spain, Israel, Canada, India, Italy, Uzbekistan, Czech Republic, South Korea and Australia. She was a featured poet of New Mirage Journal (USA) in the summer of 2011.

Alicja Kuberska is a member of the Polish Writers Associations in Warsaw, Poland and IWA Bogdani, Albania. She is also a member of directors' board of Soflay Literature Foundation.

The River Ganges

Colors ripen in the hot sun of India and merge into the
landscape.
Sky is azure and petals of red flowers are similar to the
pulsing blood.
Emeralds, hidden among the leaves, shine and water
glistens like silver.
Even the roadside dust, swirling in the air, changes into
particles of gold.

The sacred river Ganga was born in an ice cave at the base
of the Himalayas.
She defeated the Silwalik Mountains to connect with the
Brahmaputra river.
The holy river spreads widely her seven thick tresses in the
basin.
Imprisoned by Śiva in her hair, she breaks away from this
jail.

Where millions of water droplets drip onto the soil from
her blue sari,
The goddess leaves traces of her bare feet in the barren
fields.
For centuries, she gives a promise of eternal salvation
And as a good mother generously offers people the gift of
fecund land.

Poem for peace

I will build a bridge made of sentences
And I will fasten it with positive thoughts.

I will use words " *warmth and understanding",*
Later I will add my mother's prayers.

I will replace the lies of war's propaganda
With stanzas about *friendship and love.*

Next I will paint precise words
"Kindness and tolerance".

Strangers will be connected firmly
With rivets of powerful emotions.

Poem for peace, stronger than steel,
is free and immortal.

Prescription for a poem

It is not easy to write a poem.
You have to gather your thoughts
swirling quickly like snowflakes during a blizzard.
Catch them before they melt and disappear into oblivion.
Later add fever of feelings and strength of emotion .
Decorate your sentences with your dreams collected
from the silver dust of falling stars.

You can also
 pick out a melancholy longing from the bottom of the lake
and hang it on eyelashes to shine with tears
Then collect the wet haze of sadness
shimmering like drops of dew on calamus,
add grayness of the November' s landscape
Season it with a bit of bitterness and regret

Or you can
Capture the laughter suspended by an echo
between high mountain peaks.
Catch the merry words in the net of butterflies
carried by the warm breath of the wind.
Turn the rainbow over to add a smile to the sky.
Sprinkle it with a touch of humor and joy.

Finally, crazy metaphors must be released.
Let them draw colors from the imagination,
that the poem would acquire a transparent lightness
and like a soup bubble rise above everyday life.
Allow it to fly off in an unknown direction.

Jackie
Davis
Allen

Jackie Davis Allen, otherwise known as Jacqueline D. Allen or Jackie Allen, grew up in the Cumberland Mountains of Appalachia. As the next eldest daughter of a coal miner father and a stay at home mother, she was the first in her family to attend and graduate from college. Her siblings, in their own right, are accomplished, though she is the only one, to date, that has discovered the gift of writing.

Graduating from Radford University, with a Bachelors of Science degree in Early Education, she taught in both public and private schools. For over a decade she taught private art classes to children both in her home and at a local Art and Framing Shop where she also sold her original soft sculptured Victorian dolls and original christening gowns.

She resides in northern Virginia with her husband, taking much needed get-aways to their mountain home near the Blue Ridge Mountains, a place that evokes memories of days spent growing up in the Appalachian Mountains.

A lover of hats, she has worn many. Following marriage to her college sweetheart, and as wife, mother, grandmother, teacher, tutor, artist, writer, poet and crafter, she is a lover of art and antiques, surrounding herself, always, with books, seeking to learn more.

In 2015 she authored *Looking for Rainbows, Poetry, Prose and Art*, and in 2017, *Dark Side of the Moon*. Both books of mostly narrative poetry were published by Inner Child Press and were edited by hulya n. yilmaz.

http://www.innerchildpress.com/jackie-davis-allen.php
jackiedavisallen.com

Snapshot of Bengali

Native to Bengal, in South Asia
Indo-Aryan ethnicity
Represented in these states:
Bangladesh
West Bengal
Tripura
Assam

Subgroups of the Bengali Religions
Islam the largest, then Hinduism:
Baha'is
Buddhists
Christians
Hindus
Jews
Muslim
Sikhs

Global Bengali Communities
are found in the following:
Pakistan
United States
United Kingdom
South Korea
Malaysia
Italy
Singapore
Japan
Middle East
Canada

The Artist

He sits there
In the stillness
Of passion's silence
Surrounded by the tools
Of gift and clay

He begins his work
In the early morning hours
Each and every day

His heart is filled
With love and emotion
As he begins the transformation
Of his creativity
Into a piece of art

He makes the most of the tools
With humble hands
He shapes the clay

Like a vessel, a man's gifts
And talents are meant to be used
Whether in moment of desperation
Or in moment of hesitation, never
Let anything lead you astray

So, begin now. Now is the optimal time
To pick up your tools. It is not too late
If you will only start and do your part

The Struggle II

The artist that I am resides inside of me
She's a part of who I was intended to be
She struggles to become visible
To others, not secreted inside
Where heart's passion wishes to emerge

Fear takes up residence next to me
She's the intimidator who stalks and annoys
During the day and during the night
She's the invisible agent who frustrates
Why does she choose to terrorize

The artist in me, destined to be
She's the one that inspiration seeks
She struggles to become visible to to others
Not secreted, hiding inside
So, with paint and brushes by my side
An idea begins to take shape

The artist's tools, removed from their case
On canvas with which to illustrate are now
No longer impotent; with rising motivation
I am able to fulfill possibilities
Oh, why have I ignored the gift of me

A scene out my window as at my easel I sit
With fear and intimidation vanquished
I the artist, boldly mix, then paint
A combination of passion and gift
Which with talent and tools
A vision of me, the artist, begins to appea

Tzemin
Ition
Tsai

Dr. Tzemin Ition Tsai (蔡澤民博士) was born in Tzemin Ition Tsai Taiwan, Republic of China, in 1957. He holds a Ph.D. in Chemical Engineering and two Masters of Science in Applied Mathematics and Chemical Engineering. He is an associate professor at the Asia University (Taiwan), editor of "Reading, Writing and Teaching" academic text. He also writes the long-term columns for Chinese Language Monthly in Taiwan.

He is a scholar with a wide range of expertise, while maintaining a common and positive interest in science, engineering and literature member.

He has won many national literary awards. His literary works have been anthologized and published in books, journals, and newspapers in more than 40 countries and have been translated into more than a dozen languages.

Like The Flame Be Separated

Dense hilly rainforests blocking high in front of my eyes.
Home of the Bengal tiger,
Covering my unreachable attempts,
Screening out my inevitable myth,
In the profoundly sensitive, fresh and beautiful verse of
Gitanjali.

From now on, I doubt if I can
Then light step in that spiritual and mercurial poetry of the
Bard of Bengal.
The Home and the World.
Unnatural contemplation indulge in naturalism.
Peripatetic litterateur owes me an answer.
When the north wind blows to the surface of the sea,
I unfold my tempted wings in time,
Puest for knowledge so intense even under a street light.
Maybe wait until the north wind of the Bay of Bengal
blows again,
Jarul boat will be far to near,
Seagulls screaming and flying around,
The one-stringed string and sad voice of ektara is calling,
Birds all around me shine;
I drink thy sweet, thy precious word,
I kneel before thy shrine!

The Swaying Shadows Of Hibiscus Flowers

You obviously knew
My tantalizing face will never survive over tonight
Who will tell me
Why I can only have such a short youth
As true as your true love
Even if my beauty
Gradually withered tomorrow
Anyway
I was never at all willing to
Let my dark red flowers drift along with the water

You obviously knew
My heartily laugh will never survive over tonight
Who will tell me
Why my silhouette is no longer pretty and charming
Could it be that
You can't wait for my beauty
Grow old slowly
Anyway
I was never at all willing to
Let my dark red flowers hang on the branches alone

Why was the drizzle always with a mist?
I really want to hide in the wall of someone's home
To find a place for
The thought that has long been buried in my heart
Never worry about the night passing so fast
Never want to worry again
My attractive beauty
My deep laugh
My heart
Withered so quickly

In That Winter Without Red Flowers Embellishment

That two Poinsettias
which I took home from the market last year
Use flushed faces to give me a warm return
In those whistling cold days
At the moment of the cold flow left one by one
That reluctant friendship
Make me can't bear to abandon them
But this saved and at the same time harmed them

How can I know?
It would be a warm winter this year
The sun is not
as beautiful as the autumn sunset
But the heat did not reduce much
Look forward to the cold
The footsteps of the chill
Came so lazy
Let It is so warm always
The strength is so weak
That winter we looking forward to an entire year

Both of them couldn't wait
One past away in the fall and winter alternation
One survive but only a handful of green leaves left
Not a red flower bloom out
I can only touch the remaining branches
Can't find the reason to judge
It is a disaster in winter
Or because of my ignorance
Ugh…

Shareef Abdur Rasheed

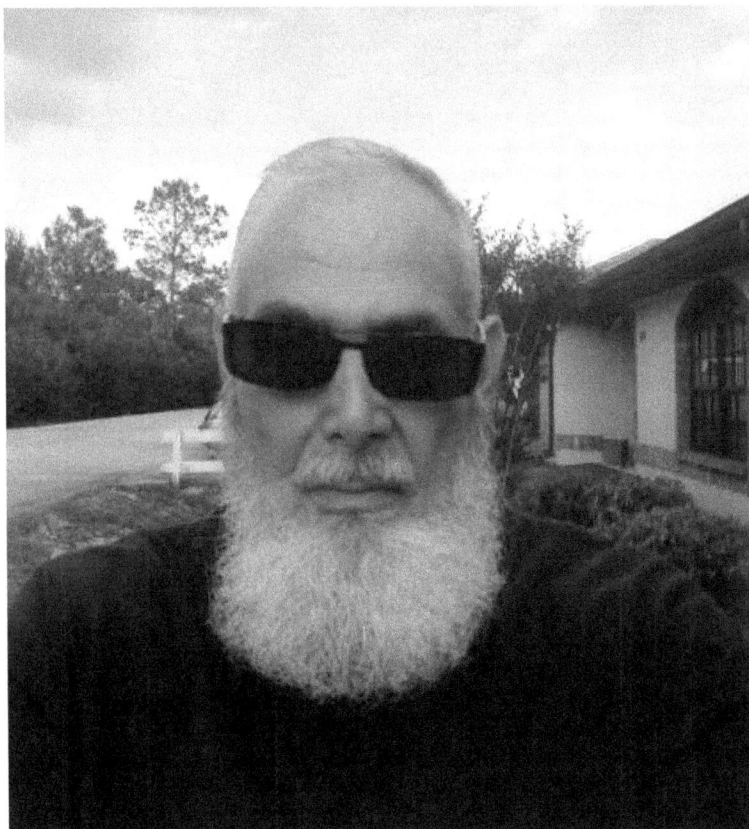

Shareef Abdur-Rasheed, AKA Zakir Flo was born and raised in Brooklyn, New York. His education includes Brooklyn College, Suffolk County Community College and Makkah, Saudi Arabia. He is a Veteran of the Viet Nam era, where in 1969 he reverted to his now reverently embraced Islamic Faith. He is very active in the Islamic community and beyond with his teachings, activism and his humanity.

Shareef's spiritual expression comes through the persona of "Zakir Flo" . Zakir is Arabic for "To remind". Never silent, Shareef Abdur-Rasheed is always dropping science, love, consciousness and signs of the time in rhyme.

Shareef is the Patriarch of the Abdur-Rasheed Family with 9 Children (6 Sons and 3 Daughters) and 41 Grandchildren (24 Boys and 17 Girls).

For more information about Shareef, visit his personal FaceBook Page at :

https://www.facebook.com/shareef.abdurrasheed1
https://zakirflo.wordpress.com

Bang, bang

la desh
Bangladesh where is the love,
concern, willingness to learn
raw poverty explored?
thus i implore, thus i implore
show your love forever more
so you ask " to whom, to whom?"
to your Bengali family from
another womb
Embroiled in famine,
flooding, constant calamity
made the great, late Beatle
George Harrison sing
Bangladesh, Bangladesh
Bengali people's present and
past woven into human fabric
as us all a thread in the magnificent
quilt
thus, us laden with guilt, this onus is it
who pray tell will require if you removed
the shoe that fit?
will you then go barefoot as your brother
lives
unlikely at best thus pass creator's test
and your heart, soul, bankroll....GIVE!

food4thought = education

poets know..,

see what others ignore
some see surface, others
see more
down to the core where hearts,
souls endure
so much beneath surface
like icebergs protrude
yet perhaps 5/6 remain mystery
this is human history
wrapped up in a false sense of
security
oblivious to obvious misery
dem eyez don't want to see
so, hearts remain cold, void
of empathy
seriously, pitifully, emphatically
so, poets know and expose
in rhyme and prose
love, hate, fears, smiles, tears
that flow, poets know

food4thought = education

You will not..,

attain Al- Birr
(righteousness)
until your willing to give up
that which you love.
(Qur'an:3,92)
you will not attain Al- Birr
(righteousness)
until you want for your
brother what you want for
yourself!
you will not inherit the
kingdom of heaven
if your clinging to the
earth
that which is fleeting
elusive
has no substance,
feelings, abusive
yet you strive to get
what you don't have
yet
as soon as you do
you say, "next"
because the attraction
a fleeting distraction
from acquiring what's best!
your wires crossed?
true date?
just do that!
a priority reset
to get that which
truly past the test

of time because it's
worth is timeless, priceless,
life changing, eternal
eternally rewarding
that which is truly blessed
comes connected to
Al-Birr (righteousness)

food4thought = education

Kimberly Burnham

See yourself in the pattern. As a 28-year-old photographer, Kimberly Burnham appreciated beauty. Then an ophthalmologist diagnosed her with a genetic eye condition saying, "Consider life, if you become blind." She discovered a healing path with insight, magnificence, and vision. Today, a poet and neurosciences expert with a PhD in Integrative Medicine, Kimberly's life mission is to change the global face of brain health. Using health coaching, Reiki, Matrix Energetics, craniosacral therapy, acupressure, and energy medicine, she supports people in their healing from nervous system and chronic pain issues. A current project is taking pages from medical literature and turning them into visual poetry by circling the words of the poem and coloring in the rest—recycling words into color and drawing out the poem.

http://www.NerveWhisperer.Solutions
https://www.linkedin.com/in/kimberlyburnham

Synonyms for Peace

"Sānti sainta shanti"
words of peace in Bengali or Bangla
in toned with bright colors in India and Bangladesh

Synonyms for peace
"abirōdha" or "abirodha"
is harmony
peace accord
agreement amity and friendliness

More synonyms working through
the alphabet to create
a word with a state of being
in a family and community

Abirōdha abirodh
aikya aman
chup chupí
firám khámosh kushalábasthā
mel miláp musálaha
nirasta rafāhiyat
sānti saanth saanthi sainta
salāhiyat sandhi shanti shānta
shdinti sthir sulh
susthiratá

Always carrying the feeling of peace
a nuance of appeasing or pacifying
in a word to calm
reconcile
or nudge into a state of peace

Feel Saanthi

Comfort
is it the same as peace
in Bengali "saanthi" is
peace and comfort
"saanthipoorn" calm
quiet and still

Is one comfortable and still in peace
or actively appreciating
grateful for what life offers in "saanthi"

Is one quiet when calm
or learning reading
actively figuring out
how to contribute to calm and peace

Is peace meant to make one
comfortable and quiet
or intended to be shared with the whole
global community

Imagine 80,000,000 saying
feeling breathing "saanth"
means many things
in Bengali from A to Y
again but calm
cold cool despite
fresh however
peace quiet recent slow still
though yet

May we again enjoy
the cool breeze of peace
recently slow and still
though yet calm
giving a fresh look
despite challenges

Om Shanti Peace

Multilingual "Om Shanti"
peace
"om shanti cánti śanti
shánti shaanti shanti"
peace in many languages

Sanskrit
the Rohingya people of Burma and Bengali
Caribbean Hindustani
Maithili and Nepali
peace all over Southeast Asia

"Shanti" from Ancient Sanskrit "úântiḥ"
peace rest calmness tranquility or bliss

"Om santi" in Koch spoken in Bangladesh
"santipap" in Thai Khmer and Laotian
in the Punjabi "śāntī"

"Sulha" "shanti" or "śanti"
or شانت in Sindhi
voiced in Pakistan and India

"Shánti" with nature
the green trees huffing out oxygen
ecological "shaanti"

Om "shanti" or "aman" in Marwari
"shānti" in Bhojpuri spoken in India
"shānta" in Bengali

"Aman" or "sukoon"in Urdu
"Samadhanam" in Malayalam
called out in Kerala, India and Singapore

Peace with society
cánti between human beings
selectively seeing
friends and neighbors everywhere

"Om salamti" in Hindi
"shāntatā" in Gujarati in words of India and Pakistan
"shaamti" in Kannada or Kurumba

The Assamese say "sānti" or "shanti"
sometimes droping the first letters
for "h̆ānti" or "nti" or "xanti"

"Shanti" within a spiritual peace
a sense of pride in actions
riding the flowing of emotions

"Om śāntātā" or "śāntī" in Marathi
"shanti" in Telegu
and in the Oriya of India "sānti"

"Amaithi" or "amaïdi"
or "samaadaanam" in Tamil
while mothers and fathers in Kashmiri
say "amn" "shaanti"
or "sala" or "sokh"

Environmental "aman"
encompassing them all
food shelter connection
and hoped for peace

Elizabeth E. Castillo

Elizabeth Esguerra Castillo is a multi-awarded and an Internationally-Published Contemporary Author/Poet and a Professional Writer / Creative Writer / Feature Writer / Journalist / Travel Writer from the Philippines. She has 2 published books, "Seasons of Emotions" (UK) and "Inner Reflections of the Muse", (USA). Elizabeth is also a co-author to more than 60 international anthologies in the USA, Canada, UK, Romania, India. She is a Contributing Editor of Inner Child Magazine, USA and an Advisory Board Member of Reflection Magazine, an international literary magazine. She is a member of the American Authors Association (AAA) and PEN International.

Web links:

Facebook Fan Page

https://free.facebook.com/ElizabethEsguerraCastillo

Google Plus

https://plus.google.com/u/0/+ElizabethCastillo

Bengali

Kolkata comes alive in lovely hues,
Vibrant colors, sparkling lights
Thematic, colorful pandals,
Cheerful faces anywhere
Your eyes can feast on.

Goddess Durga on a pedestal,
First practiced by Zamindar of Dinajpur
Handed down to Rajah Kangshanarayan of Taherpur
While Bhahananda Mazumdar of Nadiya,
Began the Sharadiya or Autum Durga Puja.

The Battle of Plassey in 1757
Dupleix suffered from shamefull, ill-treatment
And the victor of Arcot sought Parliamentary honours
In the Black Hole of Calcutta,
A ghastly tragedy broke, Ahmed Shah ruled the north-west.
Kazi Nazrul Islam, the Rebel Poet he was known,
A muezzin at a local mosque
Composed songs on Lord Krishna and Kali Maa
Icon of Bangla music in Ghazals
Espoused Indo-Islamic renaissance.

Shambala of the Valleys

Shambala of the valleys-
Magical rings of snow peaks
Like the dainty petals of lotus,
The mystical crystal mountain
Stands over a sacred lake.

Intricate, quaint palace-
Adorned with lapis, corals, gems, and shiny pearls
Shambhala, the Kingdom,
Where humanity's wisdom-
Is spared of destruction and corruption.

Shambhala, birthplace of Kalki Avatar,
Like Shangri-la, Siddhashman and Gyanungenge
Are only visible in a different dimension
Shambhala, where do your mysteries lie?
Guarded by the angels in hidden places.

Your hills come on too strong to the senses,
Above is your golden sky caressed by your beloved dawn
Only the pure of heart can see your majesty,
Witnessed by the ancient and earth's old races
Aryavathra, the Land of the Worthy Ones.

Echo

In my dreams of forever,
I hear an echo left by yesterday
In the still of the night,
Rattling leaves make me quiver.

While the Moon Goddess spreads her beauty,
Thy sound of a distant call
Mimicking my unspoken words,
Going against the rhythm of a flowing stream.

The singing Nightingale
Wanders through the darkness,
As the echo hypnotizes weak hearts
Bringing hymns left unsung.

Sweet echoes of yesteryears,
Taking one to the throes of the past
The sound takes to a halt at last,
When the heart decides it must let just let go.

Nizar Sartawi

Nizar Sartawi is a poet, translator, essayist, and columnist. He was born in Sarta, Palestine, in 1951. He is a member of literary and cultural organizations, including the Jordanian Writers Association (Jordan), General Union of Arab Writers (Cairo), Poetry Posse (U.S.), Inner Child Press International (U.S.), Bodgani (Belgium), and Axlepin Publishing (the Philippines). He has participated in poetry readings and international forums and festivals in numerous countries, including Jordan, Lebanon, Kosovo, Palestine, Morocco, Egypt, and India. Sartawi's poems have been translated into several languages. His poetry has been anthologized and published in many anthologies, journals, and newspapers in Arab countries, the U.S., Australia, Indonesia, Bosnia, Italy, India, the Philippines, and Taiwan.

Sartawi has published more than 20 books of poetry and poetry translation. His last poetry collection, *My Shadow,* was published in June, 2017 by Inner Child Press in the U.S.

For the last seven years, Sartawi has been working on poetry translation from English to Arabic and Arabic to English. This includes his Arabic poetry translation project, "Arab Contemporary Poets Series" in which 13 bilingual books have been published so far. He also has translated poems for a number of contemporary international poets such as, Veronica Golos, Elaine Equi; William S. Peters; Kalpna Singh-Chitnis; Nathalie Handal, Naomi Shihab Nye; Candice James; Ashok Bhargava; Santiago Villafania, Virginia Jasmin Pasalo; Rosa Jamali; Taro Aizu; Fahredin Shehu, and many others.

Anjali

A lonely figure, dark and slim,
on a kosha boat,
glides down the river
between the lush green reeds
and masses of algae.

Bodhi's heart leaps up in awe
as he glimpses an ancient temple
beyond the fog

He calmly kneels down
and presses his palms together
against his bosom,
as though he were inside a shrine.

The sun dives down
behind an ancient mound

The kosha
pushed by a gentle breeze
adjusts its course
and drifts towards the city of Bogra

.

Karatoa River

He was once a great river
revered by gods
hallowed by kings

But now
he's dwindled down
into a sluggish stream
flowing through uncaring lands
beside the road to Rangpur
mattering to himself
like a senile old god
who's grown tired of eternity

Yes, little child:
Like men and gods,
rivers age and die.

Autumn and the Olive Tree

The vengeful wind of autumn roared
threateningly
at the olive tree:
"I've come again
for you old witch
I'll unravel your dark green dress,
stitch by stich
I'll break your limbs
I'll crush your bones
until the skies hear your moans
I'll spill you blood
until the dry dirt in these fields
turns into mud."

"I know,"
 replied the thick rough trunk,
"you told me so
twelve months ago."

hülya
n.
yılmaz

Born in Turkey, hülya n. yılmaz presently serves as full-time faculty at Penn State and as the Director of Editing Services at Inner Child Press. Her academic publications dwell on literary relations between the West and the Islamic East and on gender conceptualizations within the context of Islam. Dr. yılmaz had her formal initiation as a creative writer in the U.S. Her published works include *Trance* –a tri-lingual book of poetry, *Aflame* –memoirs in verse and *An Aegean Breeze of Peace* –a poem collection she has co-authored with Demetrius Trifiatis. Poetry by hülya appeared in excess of fifty international anthologies.

hülya n. yılmaz, Ph.D.

Links

Personal Web Site
https://hulyasfreelancing.com

Personal Blog Site
https://dolunaylaben.wordpress.com/

Chandraketugarh

it was either journalism
language, culture and literature studies
or archeology
waiting for me
to learn passionately
all there was to learn . . .

how naïve of me!
learning
no matter how comprehensively done
leaves a new door to open routinely
there was not much of a knowledge supply in me
(among countless other worldly facts)
as far as the civilization of Bengal

this eastern South Asian region's tongue
spoken in today's Bangladesh and West Bengal
captured my keen attention as the 5th (or 6th) linguistic
construct
that bridges about 230 million people worldwide

the 11 vowel graphemes, each of which is termed a "vowel
letter"
representing six out of the seven core Bengali vowel
sounds
and two vowel diphthongs appealed to me in the extreme
so much so that i went on an experimental spree
on the road of my ancestors
to create the same vowel assembly for Turkish

so . . .

i opened Pandora's Box

and . . .

closed it as fast as i could

too complicated . . .

it's best to leave it alone
after all, Bengali stands its own

besides . . .

the legend of Chandraketugarh
with its story about Khana,
a famed astrologer and a medieval poet,
fascinated me much more

peeking through one door of history
into this archaeological site by Bidyadhari,
a river in West Bengal,
brought a direly-needed ray of light
upon this rapidly aging brain of mine

her poetry, after all, achieved the honor of recognition
as far as Bengali Literature's earliest documentation

thakte balad na kare chas
tar dukhta baro mas
"He who owns oxen, but does not plough,
His sorry state lasts twelve months of the year."

khanar bachan –"khana's words"
are said to have been silenced
to diminish this legendary poet's talent
yet, modern Bengali feminism shouts out loud:

hülya n. yılmaz

"Listen, o, listen!
Hark this tale of Khanaa!
In Bengal in the Middle Ages,
Lived a woman Khanaa, I sing her life.
The first Bengali woman poet.
Her tongue they severed with a knife."

khanar bachan –"khana's words"
silenced?
not at all!

her accurate astrological predictions
resonating in her poetry
may have indeed been seen as a threat
to her husband's career in the sciences
and he, his father or a hired hand
may have indeed cut off her tongue
her prodigious talent, however, do live on

khanar bachan –"khana's words"

Chandravati

born foremost for the village of Patuyari
in the Bengali land of medieval times
she is known to have dedicated her poetic work
to women of not only of Bengal

Ramayana was the name of her first epic art
it is said to continue to take countless minds
on the path of a decent enough discovery
of the continuous compositional unfolding
and historical expansion of this majestic write

is it her era of circa 1550 CE
or that of *khawnaa* –Khana
vaguely cited as "between the ninth and 12th centuries AD"
to be of greater significance?

what's the difference?

is it not a fact
that both women's universal verse
have come all the way to traverse
our equally messed-up sphere
alongside us in our so-called modern lands . . .

A Third World Country?

European history
in its culture-colonialist ignorance
classifies Bangladesh, "The Country of Bengal"
as a third world country

more power to TPTB?
no!
the powers that be
have cast enough damage into humanity

hey Europe, is it not about time
to wean yourself from your self-designated importance?
open at least one eye to the multitude of nightmares
you register in your chronicles with pride:
Chapter One, 1492
Chapter Two, 1550
Chapter Three, 1660
Chapter Four, 1754
Chapter Five, 1822
Chapter Six, 1855
Chapter Seven, 1914
Chapter Eight, 1920
Chapter Nine, 1936
Chapter Ten, 1945

who is on this list, you ask?
what on earth happened
to your self-proclaimed
superior intelligence?
fine then!
let us check together
in alphabetical order

by the way,
you must take notes along the way
to you, after all, belongs the honor
of re-writing human history
it would indeed be a pity
if your upcoming generations
got lost among our archives of accuracy

let us now proceed to see,
shall we?
who are the top-winners that be:
Belgium makes it to the list
as does United Kingdom
then enters France,
Germany,
Italy,
Japan,
The Netherlands,
Denmark-Norway,
Portugal,
Russia,
Spain
and United States

any questions?

hülya n. yılmaz

Teresa E. Gallion

Teresa E. Gallion was born in Shreveport, Louisiana and moved to Illinois at the age of 15. She completed her undergraduate training at the University of Illinois Chicago and received her master's degree in Psychology from Bowling Green State University in Ohio. She retired from New Mexico state government in 2012.

She moved to New Mexico in 1987. While writing sporadically for many years, in 1998 she started reading her work in the local Albuquerque poetry community. She has been a featured reader at local coffee houses, bookstores, art galleries, museums, libraries, Outpost Performance Space, the Route 66 Festival in 2001 and the State of Oklahoma's Poetry Festival in Cheyenne, Oklahoma in 2004. She occasionally hosts an open mic.

Teresa's work is published in numerous Journals and anthologies. She has two CDs: *On the Wings of the Wind* and *Poems from Chasing Light*. She has published three books: *Walking Sacred Ground, Contemplation in the High Desert* and *Chasing Light.*

Chasing Light was a finalist in the 2013 New Mexico/Arizona Book Awards.

The surreal high desert landscape and her personal spiritual journey influence the writing of this Albuquerque poet. When she is not writing, she is committed to hiking the enchanted landscapes of New Mexico. You may preview her work at

http://bit.ly/1aIVPNq or http://bit.ly/13IMLGh

Mosque City of Bagerhat

Antiquity credits you dear Bengali culture as a major influencer
in the fields of literature, music, shipbuilding,
art, architecture,
sports, currency, commerce, politics and cuisine.

The Mosque City of Bagerhat showcases your prowess
in architecture. The lost city built in the 15th century
was unveiled when vegetation that protected its existence

was removed exposing over 50 monuments. The faithful came
to kneel upon your dry earth then and today,
they still come to pay respects and heal the spirit.

You are now a World Heritage Site and the world comes
to marvel at your creations and acknowledge
your significant place among others in human history.

Water and Love

Approaching the waterfall
the lyrics of the water
invite me to sit.

I am grateful for the break.
Let the wet music
massage my aching lungs.

I hear echoes in the wind
telling my muse,
share these words with the world.

I soak in celestial moisture,
assimilate the sound and light
of liquid in my bones.

I must rest at this altitude.
Then I will give to the seeker
the words of water and love.

A Ghost Ranch Trail

The high desert sand is soft red
and sinks deep beneath my boots.
I raise each foot slowly toward

the reverie of sentinel rock
glazed in red, yellow and beige.
My cheeks bloat with joy.

I open my arms to embrace
the energy of this artistic walk.
Only the delightful distraction

of birds and bunnies shift
my attention for a moment
from rocks dripping color.

The freedom I feel is beyond words.
I give myself permission to giggle
out of control up this trail.

Ashok K. Bhargava

Ashok Bhargava is a poet, writer, community activist, public speaker, management consultant and a keen photographer. Based in Vancouver, he has published several collections of his poems: Riding the Tide, Mirror of Dreams, A Kernel of Truth, Skipping Stones, Half Open Door and Lost in the Morning Calm. His poetry has been published in various literary magazines and anthologies.

Ashok is a Poet Laureate and poet ambassador to Japan, Korea and India. He is founder of WIN: Writers International Network Canada. Its main objective is to inspire, encourage, promote and recognize writers of diverse genres, artists and community leaders. He has received many accolades including Nehru Humanitarian Award for his leadership of Writers International Network Canada, Poets without Borders Peace Award for his journeys across the globe to celebrate peace and to create alliances with poets, and Kalidasa Award for creative writings.

Lucent Fire

Prayer candles
fold and unfold the invincible Goddess
riding a striped Bengal tiger.
jubilant and uncontrolled
crowd slices other's flesh with elbows
dance death
dance life
in the narrow streets.
Taking out in procession
colorful images made of clay
surging
they cling like coiled cobras
hope to come out of it
enlightened in body and mind.
Chanting in a state of trance
they immerse the clay images in water
fragrant marigold petals float
while unassailable shakti drowns.

Boundless Love

Seeking passion never stops.
 Lovers always find love
rivers always find the oceans
drop by drop
after journeys through mountains
plains and deserts of thousands of miles
to merge and to vanish.

Love is to the lover what the lover is to love
like a seed to a flower a flower to a seed.

Time is a messenger of love
it is an angel that resides inside the hearts.

You can't own it just feel it through the senses:
touch, smell, taste, sight and sound.

Desires are the oceans
waiting for rivers to come in a colorful procession of waves
to rise like the lips to kiss to infuse celestial taste.

Love is life
its genesis, radiance
and creation: a river
seeking its lover.

Infinite Time

I will show you the origin
of the endless time
where the darkness can't be
separated from light
and it can be seen only through
the change of seasons,
spring buds
summer blossoms
autumn leaves and
wrinkled winter skins.

The nature of time
is not loneliness but companionship.
Exhale the isolation
stretch hands, catch the light,
inhale love
unfold the doors of your heart and
let feet dance to the tunes of life,
to the fragrance of passion.

Caroline
'Ceri Naz'
Nazareno

Caroline Nazareno-Gabis a.k.a. Ceri Naz, born in Anda, Pangasinan known as a 'poet of peace and friendship', is a multi-awarded poet, journalist, editor, publicist, linguist, educator, and women's advocate.

Graduated cum laude with the degree of Bachelor of Elementary Education, specialized in General Science at Pangasinan State University. Ceri have been a voracious researcher in various arts, science and literature. She volunteered in Richmond Multicultural Concerns Society, TELUS World Science, Vancouver Art Gallery, and Vancouver Aquarium.

She was privileged to be chosen as one of the Directors of Writers Capital International Foundation (WCIF), Member of the Poetry Posse, one of the Board of Directors of Galaktika ATUNIS Magazine based in Albania; the World Poetry Canada and International Director to Philippines; Global Citizen's Initiatives Member, Association for Women's rights in Development (AWID) and Anacbanua. She has been a 4th Placer in World Union of Poets Poetry Prize 2016, Writers International Network-Canada ''Amazing Poet 2015'', The Frang Bardhi Literary Prize 2014 (Albania), the sair-gazeteci or Poet-Journalist Award 2014 (Tuzla, Istanbul, Turkey) and World Poetry Empowered Poet 2013 (Vancouver, Canada).

minaret

remembering the bengali fest

upholding the sky's promise

as tall as the minaret's

lofty trademarks

where the posts are deposits

of strength,

beyond fasting and sacrifice,

are fervent prayers

in a dome of faith.

The Home and The World

I would like to meet Tagore

In my home, in a temporary haven,

In a Wanderlust or destiny places;

If this is the perfect time

To be enlightened by his social reforms,

I will sing my poetry and his poems

In luminous height;

And if he listens to me,

I can make a legend,

For I found a world I have to live.

Nirja
Lotus Flower; Goddess Laxmi

instant dimiurgic flair,

despite the clouds

that signal heavenly pour

i come to you,

because you are alone,

you think of me,

un-isolated,

you invited me

as your special guest

in a loop full of memories

like a celestial bloom

where i am about to plant;

by seeing you,

i am recreated,

beyond happiness

Swapna
Behera

Swapna Behera is a bilingual contemporary poet, author, translator and editor from Odisha, India.She was a teacher from 1984 to 2015 . Her stories, poems and articles are widely published in National and International journals, and ezines, and are translated into different national and International languages. She has penned four books. She was conferred upon the Prestigious International Poesis Award of Honor at the 2nd Bharat Award for Literature as Jury in 2015, The Enchanting Muse Award in India World Poetree Festival 2017, World Icon of Peace Award in 2017, and the Pentasi B World Fellow Poet in 2017.. She is the recipient of Gold Cross Of Wisdom Award ,the medal for The Best Teachers of the World from World Union of Poets in 2018, and The LIfe time Achievement Award ,The Best Planner Award and The Sahitya Shiromani Award from the Literati Cosmos Society 2018 .She is the Ambassador of Humanity by Hafrikan Prince Art World,Africa 2018 and an official member of World Nation's Writers Union ,Kazakhstan2018. At present she is the manager at Large, Planner and Columnist of The Literati and the administrator of several poetic groups

Baul –The Mystic Melody of Bengal

When religion and music entwine
From the distant Land of Vatula
A melody celebrates
As crazy as wind.
A Baul singer sings ....

The mystic nomadic minstrels
Dance and reflect joy immortal
The instruments of Dotar ,Ektar and the dugiya
You ,the Bauls of Bengal
The caravans of Bhakti movement and Sufi
You shower your feelings
Your songs induce Rabindra Sangit
Expresses gauge and harmony
Religious beliefs and imagery
Human body the paramount
Theme of Baul school
 Life is significant
Nothing before or after
Bauls the heterogeneous
group of many sects
Where all streams confluence
Hindus, sufis and muslims
For them
No heaven ,no salvation
No documents, history or origin
When souls sing
Rhythm of dhol and cymbals
Anklets with bells of ghungur
When music is the religion
The Intangible cultural heritage
Their saffron robes and belts

Lalon Akrah or Parvati Baul
The nomadic song lingers
In the ears as the eternal song of harmony
Forever and ever ....

The Last Decipher Of The Bullet

The Bullet on the martyr's chest
Cries ,suffocates with panacea of blood
The iron cylinder screeches
Take me out ,take me out
I too die with this man
The numismatic hatred
The cruelty and vengeance
The destructive deduction
The sadist plan of a few
The metabolic death of an anatomy

The bullet appeals
"Make me a ballot oh ! Lord
I wish to win the hearts
And not be a prisoner in the ventricles of the heart
I can't be a slave of Lucifer
Washed away with the over flooded tears
The agony of death kills me every second
Melt my iron body
To make a tiller
To grow more and more
The planet needs food
And never streams of blood !!!!........

Aroma

Aroma of life
Moments in Paradise

Aroma of love
The bark of nimbus

Aroma of sorrow
The domain of ego

Aroma of words
The voyage of the dictum

Aroma of emotions
The legitimate rainbows

Aroma of fear
Royal escorts of the track

Aroma of lust
Intent vicious passion

Aroma of light
May be melting self silently - - -

......

Swapna Behera

88

William S. Peters Sr.

Bill's writing career spans a period of over 50 years. Being first Published in 1972, Bill has since went on to Author in excess of 40 additional Volumes of Poetry, Short Stories, etc., expressing his thoughts on matters of the Heart, Spirit, Consciousness and Humanity. His primary focus is that of Love, Peace and Understanding!

Bill says . . .

I have always likened Life to that of a Garden. So, for me, Life is simply about the Seeds we Sow and Nourish. All things we "Think and Do", will "Be" Cause and eventually manifest itself to being an "Effect" within our own personal "Existences" and "Experiences" . . . whether it be Fruit, Flowers, Weeds or Barren Landscapes! Bill highly regards the Fruits of his Labor and wishes that everyone would thus go on to plant "Lovely" Seeds on "Good Ground" in their own Gardens of Life!

to connect with Bill, he is all things Inner Child

www.iaminnerchild.com

Personal Web Site

www.iamjustbill.com

Bengali

We are a people
We are a land

We speak in a language
Of diversity
And have done so
For many a year

From Bangladesh
To West Bengal
We exude many colors,
Many tongues
Many means
Of worshipping
The Creator
Of all things

We were once called
The Vedda from Sri Lanka
And later we embrace the
Mediterranean peoples
Who spoke Indo-European languages . . .
We did not mind
For they too
Became one of us,
For we were strong

In the 8th century we welcomed
Peoples of Arab, Turkish, and Persian descent
As they migrated
To our lands . . .
We embraced

One and another
And called ourselves
The Bengali

Today,
We stand
As one,
For one
For us all

Divinely Flawed

I live in a world of poetry,
Words,
Inspiration,
Love,
And . . .
Energy

My medium is words,
Which I so love
Study,
Create, Kwee-Ate, Qweate
And seek to hone
That I may convey
The beauty
And other
Of what I see,
Or at least think I see

Everywhere I look,
When i look,
I see poetry
Dancing,
Prancing
Lifting her skirts
That I may get a peek
At the undergarments
Of truth . . .
Sometimes they are absent
And "Truth" nakedly exposes
All of her grandeur

Some times I can bear it,
But most times I can not,
For "Truth" is stark in contrast
To the life that I live . . .
Mostly

My vanity,
My ego,
My delusion,
And the illusions
Oft times
Shade her light
To look other than what
"IS"

There are many lights
With all degrees of brilliance,
And a myriad of colors,
Many which are not detectable
By our empirical eyes . . .
Their vibrations are foreign
To our "Status Quo"

All of this
Comes not
Without purpose !

Flawed I proclaim,
For in what name
Do I defame
That which is Divine . . .
Mine ?

Father forgive me . . .
For I too,
Know not what
I DO !

I must admit not
That I am "Divinely Flawed"
And thus I am awed
By the perfection
Of it all

My mind is imperial
And I subtly seek to colonize
My thought,
My experience,
My perspectives
To fit
Borrowed paradigms
That are not that of mine own.

If you can not be the Poet . . . Be the Poem ! ~ unknown

Singularity

I climbed that mountain
Named 'Glory'
Where 'Blessing'
Lived upon its peaks
And speaks
Of the wonder
Of all creation

The struggle was arduous,
But my soul was not familiar
With defeat

I scraped,
I clawed,
I fought,
I weathered the storms,
I endured
By the grace
Of my Creator

Finally ...

As I stood upon the precipice
Of my achievement
I look upon the valleys
From whence I come
And I saw
Greater things before me

Is not life beautiful?

Endless possibilities...
Open thine eye!

Singularity .... to thine self be true.

October
2018
Features

~ * ~

Alicia Minjarez

Lonneice Weeks-Badley

Lopamudra Mishra

Abdelwahed Souayah

i Fly because I Can

. . . said the Dreamer to the world.

Alicia Minjarez

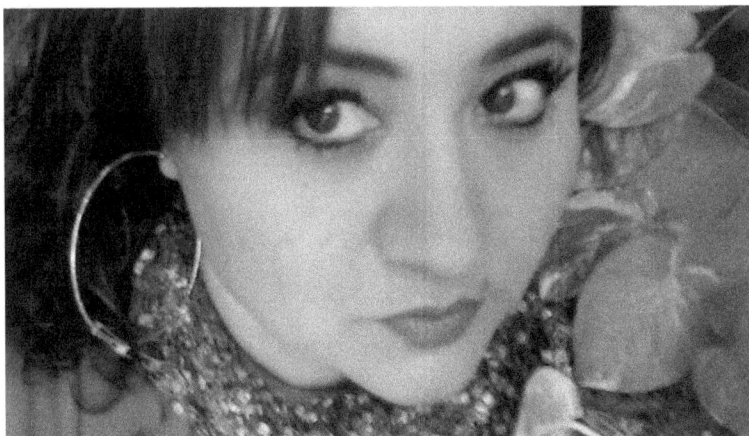

Poet, Translator, Singer, University Professor, Broadcast locution Radio and T.V.

Alicia Minjarez Ramírez was born in Tijuana, Mexico. She is an internationally renowned poetess and author who has won numerous awards including the EASAL medal by the European Academy of Sciences and Letters 2018 at Paris, France. Awarded "Pride of the Globe" WNWU, Kazakhstan 2018; Awarded "Universal Inspirational Poet", Pentasi B. World, India 2017; Winner of a special mention and a medal in the International Poetry Prize NOSSIDE Italy 2015, recognized by UNESCO. Awarded with the IWA BOGDANI Albania Award, 2016. Awarded with the Third Place in French Poetry in the International Poetry Prize 'Sous les traces de Léopold Sédar Senghor" at Milan, Italy, 2016 recognized by ONU and UNESCO. Winner of a mention in the NOSSIDE Poetry Prize, Italy 2016. Awarded "Universal Inspirational Poet" Pentasi B. World, Africa, Ghana 2016.

She was considered among the International Poets published on the XXI Century World Literature Book released at New Delhi, India, 2016. Her poems have been translated into: English, Albanian, French, Cameroonian, Arabic, Azerbaijan, Turkish, Chinese, Taiwanese, Portuguese, Polish and Italian. And published in more than 90 International Anthologies, journals and magazines around the world.

TRAVELER

Redemptive breeze
imprisons my space,
like raining stars
as fragrant words
at the crescent moon,
salt conspires about
your shooting and lasting
existence.

Blue air flutter about
your wet
vertices notes,
ascending
through
the tree's essence.
Guttural sounds
spotting
the horizon.

I sense you
among murmurs
of leaves
diluting
liquid shadows,
imaginary
pigeon's pieces,
luminance music
of the dreams
we forge.

I find you,
wrong or right,
in haste;

in the rain's
incessant voice.
Beautiful traveler
of dreamed steps
and arms of fire.

Drowned in
desire-scented steam
I dusk upon
foreign oaks,
as touch produced by
your path;
dark moor
of an old sky
reinvent
your word of light,
the illusory
copulation
of language.

IT RAINS…

A longing breeze
tries to show itself,
like nostalgia
migrating
up in the air.

Water permeates
my body.
Your breath
fills in
the context.

Longing secrets
that the wind
shakes up in the offing,
then nothingness.

I walk behind
upon the moisture
left by the drops
under the branches.

Birds get detached
from their nests,
looking for
the promised shelter.

Church bells ring,
outside
the night
interrupts.
I long to dry off

the rain,
like those birds
besetting
park trees
in the evening.

The stillness of your eyes
invades me…
Ecstatic wings,
paralyzing their flight.
At my silence's feet.

THE PATH OF YOUR STEPS

Naked and lurking
tenderness
at the riverbank,
a kiss clinging on
as a vine
and climbing
through the sap
of my branches.

I spy on the night
in your thistles,
adjacent meridians
in the nectar
of your Nile.

Of all your summers
emanate and disappear
crepuscular fragments,
frosts decorate
the melodic chant
of orioles
and blackbirds.

I invent you and lose you
in the zephyr choleric notes,
the sublime lightness
makes silence thunder up.

Dissolving my dawns
in the hustle of memory,
fire against the light
of the stranger and nubile
torso of your body.

You rain and crumble
over my fragrant touch,
blast that exalts
the sound of the stones
building up
my roads,
long gone
and desolated
landscapes
blooming today
behind your
own steps.

Alicia Minjarez

Lonneice Weeks-Badley

Lonneice Weeks-Badley was born to Oliver and Margaret in New York.

Resides in Manning South Carolina and is a mother of two daughters, the proud grandmother of three grandsons, one granddaughter and one great granddaughter.

I am an Author, Chaplain, Minister, Intercessor of the LORD; Owner of Rajahne's Gifted Hands at Work/Inspired Books. I love poetry; two of my books have been published by Bill Peters-Inner Child Press and Team. The Year of the Poet inspired me to press on. It's an honor to announce my first children's book is coming out this summer.

A FREE Being

A FREE Being is who you were
Created in the image of God
Then satan came on the scene
And polluted Humanity
My Only begotten Son
Was sent on the scene
For everyone to become
A FREE Being
He was called by various
Dialects, tongues or idioms
Jesus is His name
And always will be
One in the same to everyone
A FREE Being
FREE from our infirmities and sins
What was and still is His desires
For us to feel and see
The great works of He
A FREE Being
Is a Believer who trusted in Me
To help them to become FREE in the mind
FREE in the spirit as the Holy Spirit hear it
FREE in the heart to share My love
And to be FREE living in the new talk,
Walk and lifestyle
Continuously being blessed
With what was left within ...
A FREE Being

Hearts of LOVE for Humanity

Hearts of LOVE for Humanity
Comes from GOD, who LOVES so deep
People wake up ---out of your sleep
You have been set free…
My LOVE is in the middle of thee
Connecting your mind and Me (Breath of God)
Together we're one ---just believe

Hearts of LOVE for Humanity

Can you share a penny, nickel, dime,
quarter or dollar; if you please…
Don't turn and run from me
Please hear my plea
Some of us are NOT out here to lie
and steal from you; I'm homeless
And know NOT what to do
I need help to eat

Hearts of LOVE for Humanity

Oh what a great relief it'll be
To give back expecting nothing in return
For that person ---could have been me…
Thanks for sharing your compassionate heart
And Me (LOVE) who's imbedded
You helped one that was down and blue
As you give back---to humanity.

Hearts of LOVE for Humanity

Proudly they can acknowledge;
Someone DOES care for me…

Hearts of LOVE for Humanity
Each One ~ Reach One
Each One ~ Teach One
To give and LOVE as HE
Love and Peace….

Piece above is from "The Essence of God's Law of Love"

THE ESSENCE of GOD'S LAW of LOVE

The Essence of God's Law of Love
Demonstrates Him deep inside of us
It's told in the beginning
The bible speaks His truth
This is NOT new news
This is what the LORD is sending

The Essence of God's Law of Love
So we can all grow
In His Great Law of Love
As He tells us so
There's no condescending
Of another—
My LOVE is never ending
Just do this for me

The Essence of God's Law of Love
Fear (respect) the LORD your **God**,
Walk in all His ways
Love Him; every day,
Serve Him; as you pray,
Guess what else you can do
Share what He gave to you
Unconditional Love; that's so true
with family, friends and strangers too

The Essence of God's Law of Love
Can you do this for me?
With all your heart and with all your soul
For this is my breathtaking and ultimate goal; ever told
My Law of Love will always live in Him and Him in Me
For this is The Essence of God's Law of Love
Inside He that BELIEVE...

Lonneice Weeks-Badley

Lopamudra Mishra

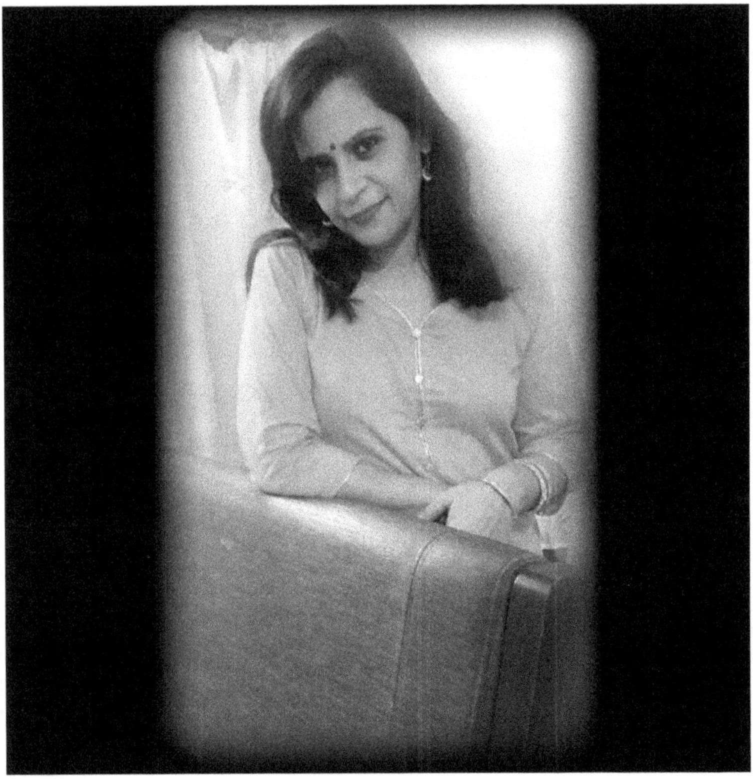

Lopamudra Mishra,native puri,now residing inBhubaneswa r Orissa, She completed her graduation {English Hons} from Sailabala Women's college Cuttack, And post – graduation {English} from Ravenshaw University Cuttack. Her fascination for writing came from her grandfather and father from an early age. Writing for her is the powerful medium of expression.Her poems have been published in many magazines and anthologies. Her first book "Rhyme Of Rain" was published in march 2017, second book "First Rain" in August 2017 and her third book "Tingling Parables" in May 2018.

Heap Of Stones

Standing beside the debris,
Of sand stones,
Started counting each stone,
From top to bottom,
One by one measured the thickness,
Its intensity and depth of hardcore,
Each brick sings
The tone of treachery
And betrayal,
My wobbling steps cry,
This is not fair.
Why am I to be punished ?
Why this warfare?
The seeds I planted,
With lots of hope,
Dried in the hot sun.
My feet could feel the pinch of hard rocks,
The dust in the air ,
Cloud my goal,
My eyes lack tears,
Blinks time to time,
Reminding me,
Time has come ,
To purify the atmosphere,
But... I am helpless,
I cannot do anything,
Except from standing near the heap of stones

What are you for me ?

For you I may be a dew,
That sparkles in sunlight
And vanishes in brighter hue,
Aha! for me ,
You are my day ,
My blazing star,
I fabricate tales of romance,
Keeping you as my prime star cast,
Your presence filled the barren groove,,
Colouring me and my surrounding with your dazzling
shadow,,
From my secret chamber I whisper your name,
Engrave it through my fountain pen,
You know my depressed state,
Yet dispassionate regarding my health,
Is not a joke?
My dear ,you reign my brain,
Every where I visualise your traces,
Mistaken ...
Then move ahead ,
Carrying you in my heart,
You run in neurons,
Hence you activates my electrons,
Now you are far away,
Keeping me waiting.

Presentiments

I see the dancing blue cloud,
In the immeasurable upper atmosphere,
When I measured the depth,
From its space to my breath,
The extensive miles that I assess,
Is thousand light year or above,

Yet ,I feel the hot inhale and exhale air,
Being settled miles away,
Yes ,this is my presentiments,
I am connected to your tenderness,
That the hydrogen power of brain,
Fails to receive favourably,
In the dark sky, when I find you missing,
My oblivion didn't cry,
Rather my dry tears smiles seeing your portrait,
I then associate your links to my casement,
For some moments I feel your presence,
You blink with your streak,
I forget my shriek,
I try to grasp the hours of bliss,
Now when my soul is attached to thee,
Can the fog hide you from me?

Abdelwahed Souayah

Abdelwahed Souayah (born in Bembla/Tunisia) studied Arabic Literature at the University of Sousse and later taught Arabic Language and Literature. He heads the Tunisian Writer's Association (Monastir chapter) and ranks among the principal characters who firmly established modern literature in his country, often referred to as »Mouvement du texte«. He has published widely in local and international literary magazines and has participated in multiple radio and television broadcasts. Souayah has authored five volumes of prose poetry and also writes short stories, literary criticism, as well as scholarly essays. Current publication: »I write for the tree « (2017, Badaoui-Verlag).

Child

Every day, I play. Sometimes I buy myself ice cream

and a box of chocolates.

I ponder upon stories and have been flooded

with messages.

My new wardrobe for the celebration makes me happy.

I piss at the city wall.

And I kiss the leftover bread goodbye before I throw it out.

Not you, but I have lost a tooth

and now I am asking the Gazelle

to give me one of hers.

I bend over my bed each night

and dream of Shakira ….

After so many years, I have discovered that I am a child.

This Cursed Thing

He follows me and follows my shadow

He eats and drinks with me.

He takes hold of my bed without even taking a bath

or taking his shoes off

Sour stench of his breath

Groans during every cold

Within his body there is the smell of the sea

Traces of urine in his underwear.

The songs past midnight

His conspicuous demands while shaving down there

His masturbations

Surrounded by cigarette butts scattered about

When he beds me, he is always fierce.

Because of him I need to see the physician once a day

My body, yes, this dammed body.

Nudity

The wind crashes through distant valleys
my ruins are traversed by insane ocean trees
eyes, gazing, are falling upon me
and my love has awakened again
the madness has returned
All of you, staring at me
you touch my brow and inscribe
your eyes upon it
you are collecting from me crowns and paintings
the traces of many footsteps
this new drawing of the universe
be there when my hand
hovers over the body pausing and exploring
listen to the language of the fish
the entire shore needs witnesses
and the rose is smiling along
wants to be seen

I am still a dreamer
who sees her and oneself
you will find my miracles in my adventures
and words
believe me when I say that thunder
means that the sky is laughing
while birthing dew

translated Into english by Paul-Henri Campbell

Inner Child Press
News

We are so excited to announce the New and upcoming books of some of our Poetry Posse authors.

On the following pages we present to you ...

Jackie Davis Allen

Gail Weston Shazor

hülya n. yılmaz

Nizar Sartawi

Faleeha Hassan

Caroline 'Ceri' Nazareno

William S. Peters, Sr.

Now Available at
www.innerchildpress.com

Now Available at
www.innerchildpress.com

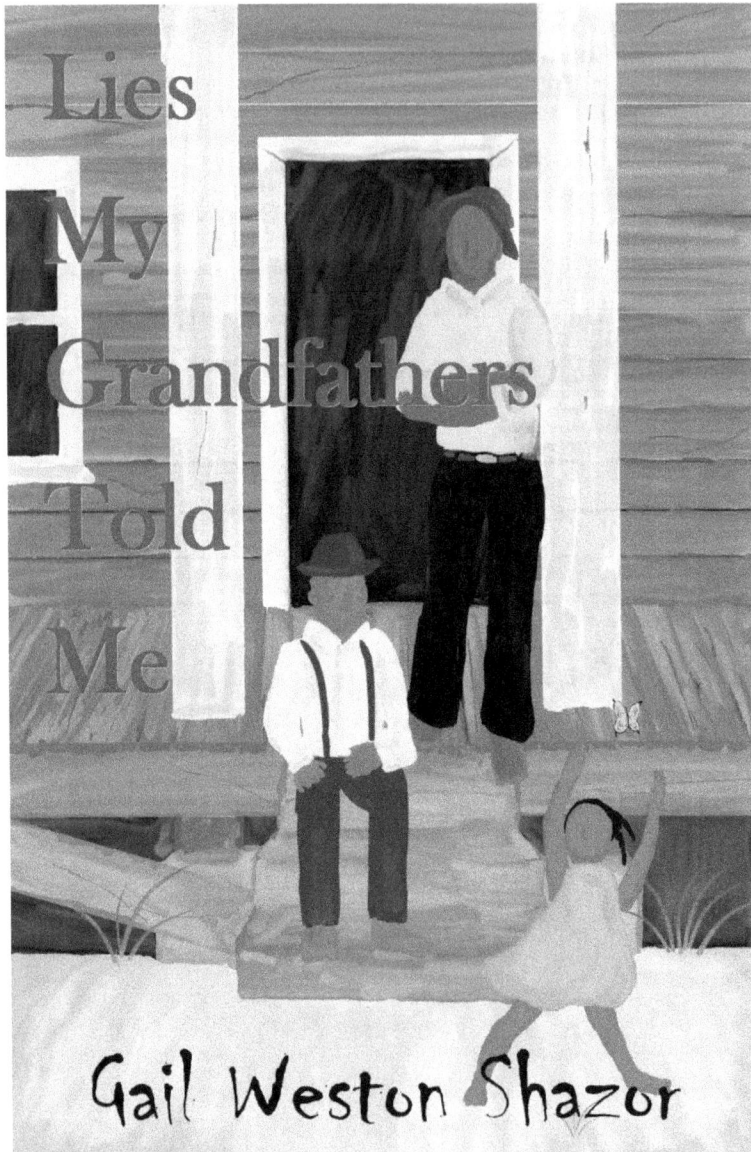

Lies My Grandfathers Told Me

Gail Weston Shazor

Now Available at
www.innerchildpress.com

Aflame

Memoirs in Verse

hülya n. yılmaz

Inner Child Press News

Now Available at
www.innerchildpress.com

My Shadow

Nizar Sartawi

Now Available at
www.innerchildpress.com

Mass Graves

Faleeha Hassan

Now Available at
www.innerchildpress.com

Breakfast

for

Butterflies

Faleeha Hassan

Now Available at

www.innerchildpress.com

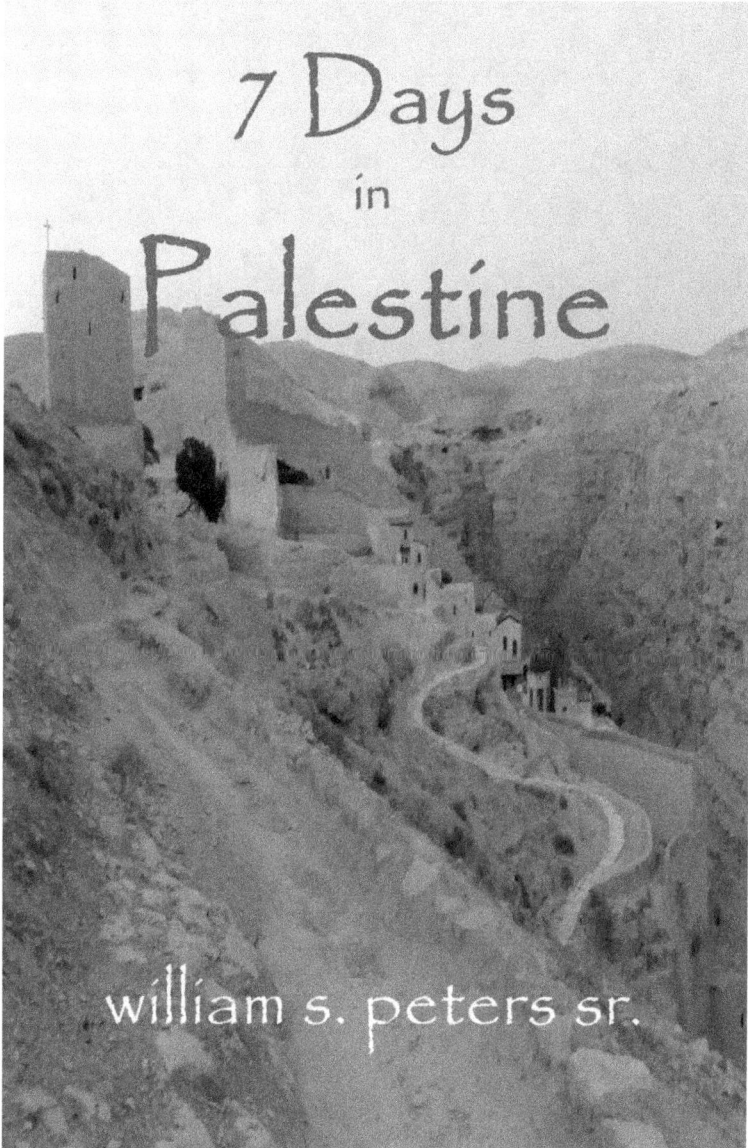

7 Days in Palestine

william s. peters sr.

Now Available at
www.innerchildpress.com

inner child press
presents

Tunisia My Love

william s. peters, sr.

Coming in December of 2018

The Journey

Footprints and Shadows

Kosovo

Tunisia

Macedonia

Morocco

Jordan

Palestine

Israel

Italy

Turkey

a collection of poetry inspired during my travels

william s. peters, sr.

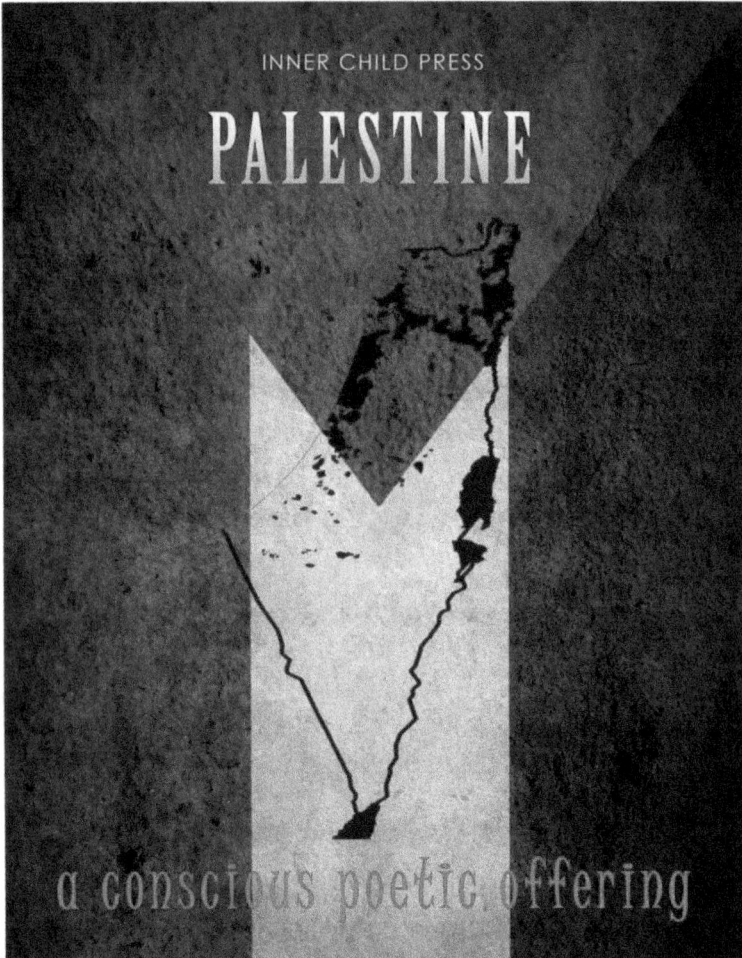

INNER CHILD PRESS

PALESTINE

a conscious poetic offering

Now Available at
www.innerchildpress.com

Now Available at
www.innerchildpress.com

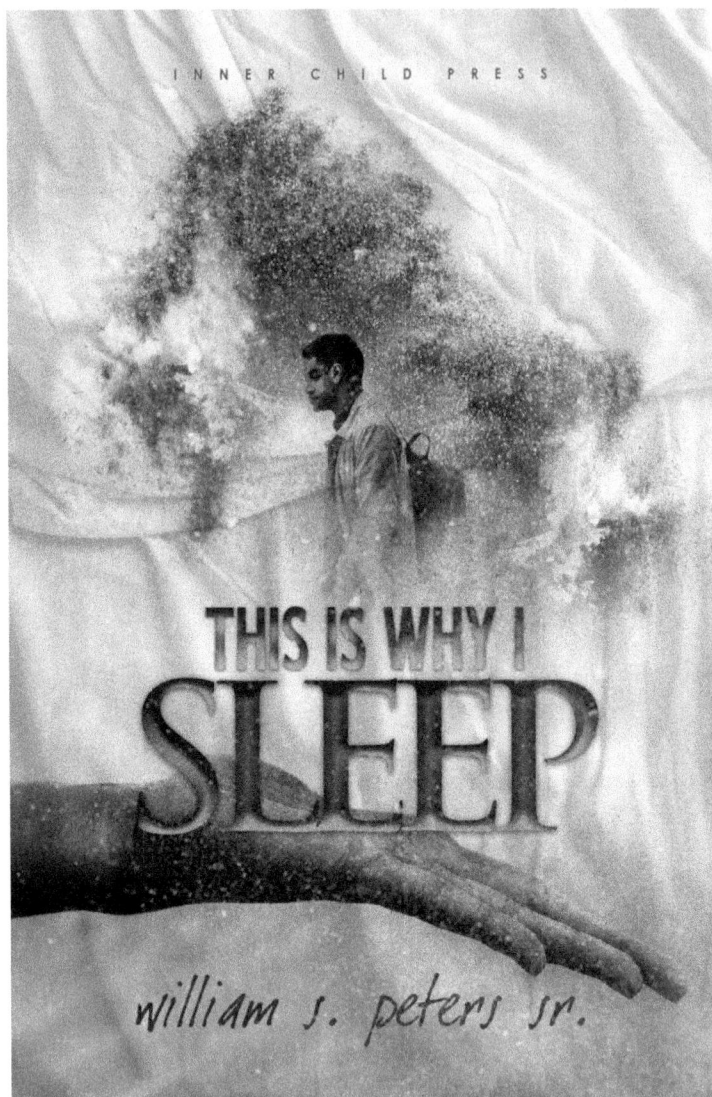

INNER CHILD PRESS

THIS IS WHY I
SLEEP

william s. peters sr.

Now Available at
www.innerchildpress.com

Inward Reflections

Think on These Things
Book II

william s. peters, sr.

Now Available at
www.innerchildpress.com

Poetry from the Balkans

The Balkan Poets

Other

Anthological

works from

Inner Child Press, ltd.

www.innerchildpress.com

janet

gone too soon . . .

Now Available

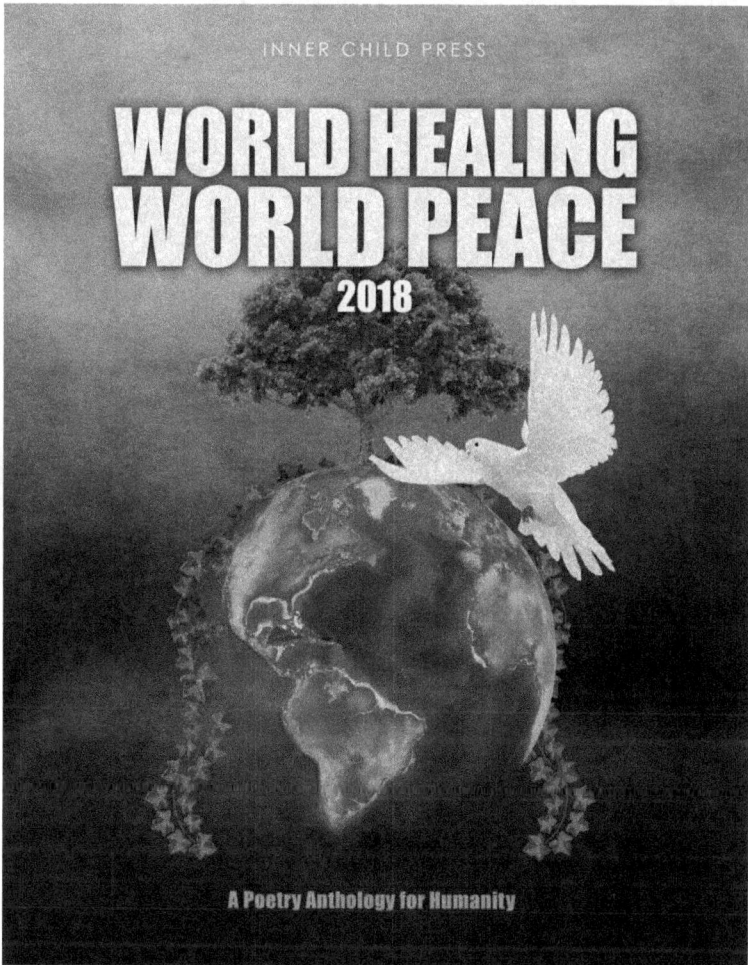

INNER CHILD PRESS

WORLD HEALING WORLD PEACE
2018

A Poetry Anthology for Humanity

Now Available

www.worldhealingworldpeacepoetry.com

Now Available

www.worldhealingworldpeacepoetry.com

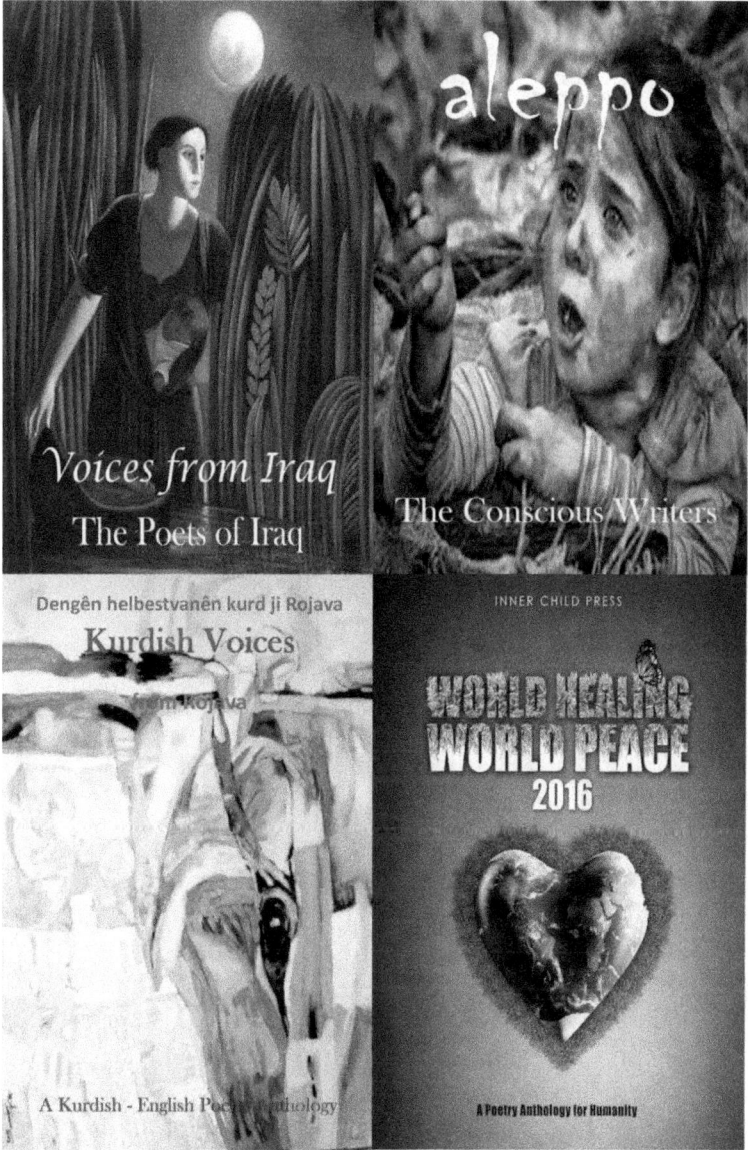

Voices from Iraq
The Poets of Iraq

aleppo
The Conscious Writers

Dengên helbestvanên kurd ji Rojava
Kurdish Voices
from Rojava

A Kurdish - English Poetry Anthology

INNER CHILD PRESS

WORLD HEALING
WORLD PEACE
2016

A Poetry Anthology for Humanity

Now Available

www.innerchildpress.com/anthologies

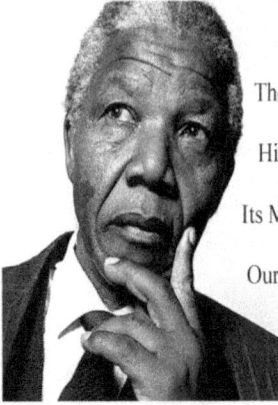

Mandela

The Man

His Life

Its Meaning

Our Words

Poetry . . . Commentary & Stories
The Anthological Writers

A GATHERING OF WORDS

POETRY & COMMENTARY
FOR

TRAYVON MARTIN

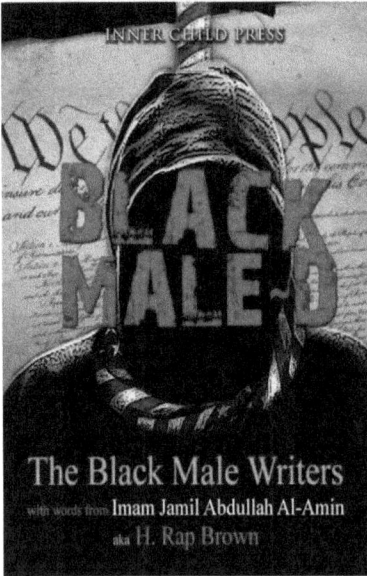

INNER CHILD PRESS

BLACK MALE-D

The Black Male Writers
with words from Imam Jamil Abdullah Al-Amin
aka H. Rap Brown

Now Available

www.innerchildpress.com/anthologies

Now Available

www.innerchildpress.com/anthologies

healing through words

Poetry ... Prose ... Prayer ... Stories

Janet
gone too soon . . .

a
Poetically
Spoken
Anthology
volume 1
Collector's Edition

The Poetry Posse
Presents

an anthology
of

Love

The Poetry Posse 2016

Now Available

www.innerchildpress.com/anthologies

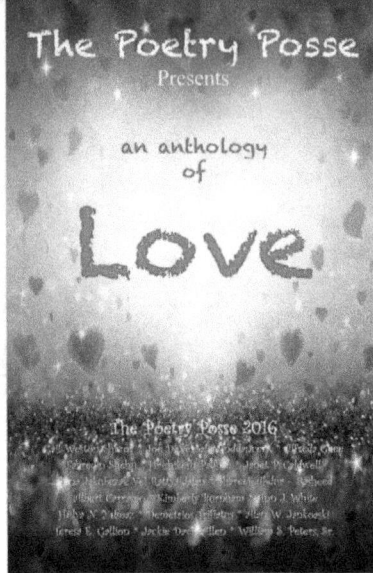

i want my
PoEtRy
to . . .

a collection of the Voices of Many inspired by . . .

Monte Smith

a collection of the Voices of Many inspired by . . .

Monte Smith

i want my
PoEtRy
to . . .

volume II

i want my
PoEtRy
to . . .   volume 3

a collection of the Voices of Many inspired by . . .

Monte Smith

11 Words

(9 lines . . .)

for those who are challenged

an anthology of Poetry inspired by . . .

Poetry Dancer

Now Available

www.innerchildpress.com/anthologies

The Year of the Poet
January 2014

The Poetry Posse

Jamie Bond
Gail Weston Shazor
Albert 'Infinite' Carrasco
Siddartha Beth Pierce
Janet P. Caldwell
June 'Bugg' Barefield
Debbie M. Allen
Tony Henninger
Joe DaVerbal Minddancer
Robert Gibbons
Neetu Wali
Shareef Abdur-Rasheed
William S. Peters, Sr.

Carnation

Our January Feature
Terri L. Johnson

the Year of the Poet
February 2014

The Poetry Posse

Jamie Bond
Gail Weston Shazor
Albert 'Infinite' Carrasco
Siddartha Beth Pierce
Janet P. Caldwell
June 'Bugg' Barefield
Debbie M. Allen
Tony Henninger
Joe DaVerbal Minddancer
Robert Gibbons
Neetu Wali
Shareef Abdur-Rasheed
William S. Peters, Sr.

violets

Our February Features
Teresa E. Gallion & Robert Gibson

the Year of the Poet
March 2014

The Poetry Posse

Jamie Bond
Gail Weston Shazor
Albert 'Infinite' Carrasco
Siddartha Beth Pierce
Janet P. Caldwell
June 'Bugg' Barefield
Debbie M. Allen
Tony Henninger
Joe DaVerbal Minddancer
Robert Gibbons
Neetu Wali
Shareef Abdur-Rasheed
Kimberly Burnham
William S. Peters, Sr.

Our March Featured Poets
Alicia C. Cooper & hülya yılmaz

the Year of the Poet
April 2014

The Poetry Posse

Jamie Bond
Gail Weston Shazor
Albert 'Infinite' Carrasco
Siddartha Beth Pierce
Janet P. Caldwell
June 'Bugg' Barefield
Debbie M. Allen
Tony Henninger
Joe DaVerbal Minddancer
Robert Gibbons
Neetu Wali
Shareef Abdur-Rasheed
Kimberly Burnham
William S. Peters, Sr.

Our April Featured Poets
Fahredin Shehu
Martina Reisz Newberry
Justin Blackburn
Monte Smith

Sweet Pea

celebrating international poetry month

Now Available

www.innerchildpress.com/the-year-of-the-poet

the year of the poet
May 2014

May's Featured Poets
ReeCee
Joski the Poet
Shannon Stanton

Dedicated To our Children

The Poetry Posse
Jamie Bond
Gail Weston Shazor
Albert 'Infinite' Carrasco
Siddartha Beth Pierce
Janet P. Caldwell
Jackie 'Bugg' Barnfield
Debbie M. Allen
Tony Henninger
Joe DaVerbal Minddancer
Robert Gibbons
Neetu Wali
Shareef Abdur-Rasheed
Kimberly Burnham
William S. Peters, Sr.

Lily of the Valley

the Year of the Poet
June 2014

Love & Relationship

Rose

June's Featured Poets
Shamelle McLin
Jacqueline D. E. Kennedy
Abraham S. Benjamin

The Poetry Posse
Jamie Bond
Gail Weston Shazor
Albert 'Infinite' Carrasco
Siddartha Beth Pierce
Janet P. Caldwell
Jackie 'Bugg' Barnfield
Debbie M. Allen
Tony Henninger
Joe DaVerbal Minddancer
Robert Gibbons
Neetu Wali
Shareef Abdur-Rasheed
Kimberly Burnham
William S. Peters, Sr.

The Year of the Poet
July 2014

July Featured Poets
Christene A. V. Williams
Dr. John R. Strum
Kolade Olanrewaju Freedom

The Poetry Posse
Jamie Bond
Gail Weston Shazor
Albert 'Infinite' Carrasco
Siddartha Beth Pierce
Janet P. Caldwell
Jackie 'Bugg' Barnfield
Debbie M. Allen
Tony Henninger
Joe DaVerbal Minddancer
Robert Gibbons
Neetu Wali
Shareef Abdur-Rasheed
Kimberly Burnham
William S. Peters, Sr.

Lotus
Asian Flower of the Month

The Year of the Poet
August 2014

Gladiolus

The Poetry Posse
Jamie Bond
Gail Weston Shazor
Albert 'Infinite' Carrasco
Siddartha Beth Pierce
Janet P. Caldwell
Jackie 'Bugg' Barnfield
Debbie M. Allen
Tony Henninger
Joe DaVerbal Minddancer
Robert Gibbons
Neetu Wali
Shareef Abdur-Rasheed
Kimberly Burnham
William S. Peters, Sr.

August Feature Poets
Ann White • Rosalind Cherry • Shella Jenkins

Now Available

www.innerchildpress.com/the-year-of-the-poet

The Year of the Poet
September 2014

Aster   Morning-Glory

Wild Chestnut September Birth of Flower

September Feature Poets
Florence Malone * Keith Alan Hamilton

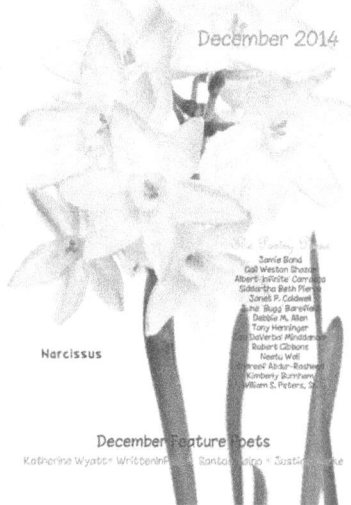

The Poetry Posse
Jamie Bond * Gail Weston Shazor * Albert Infinite Carrasco * Siddartha Beth Pierce
Janet P. Caldwell * June 'Bugg' Barefield * Debbie M. Allen * Tony Henninger
Joe DaVerbal Minddancer * Robert Gibbons * Neetu Wali * Shareef Abdur-Rasheed
Kimberly Burnham * William S. Peters, Sr.

THE YEAR OF THE POET
October 2014

Red Poppy

The Poetry Posse
Jamie Bond * Gail Weston Shazor * Albert Infinite Carrasco * Siddartha Beth Pierce
Janet P. Caldwell * June 'Bugg' Barefield * Debbie M. Allen * Tony Henninger
Joe DaVerbal Minddancer * Robert Gibbons * Neetu Wali * Shareef Abdur-Rasheed
Kimberly Burnham * William S. Peters, Sr.

October Feature Poets
Ceri Naz * RaJendra Padhi * Elizabeth Castillo

THE YEAR OF THE POET
November 2014

Chrysanthemum

The Poetry Posse
Jamie Bond * Gail Weston Shazor * Siddartha Beth Pierce
Janet P. Caldwell * June 'Bugg' Barefield * Debbie M. Allen * Tony Henninger
Joe DaVerbal Minddancer * Robert Gibbons * Neetu Wali * Shareef Abdur-Rasheed
Kimberly Burnham * William S. Peters, Sr.

November Feature Poets
Jocelyn Mosman * Jackie Allen * James Moore * Neville Hiatt

THE YEAR OF THE POET
December 2014

The Poetry Posse
Jamie Bond
Gail Weston Shazor
Albert Infinite Carrasco
Siddartha Beth Pierce
Janet P. Caldwell
June 'Bugg' Barefield
Debbie M. Allen
Tony Henninger
Joe DaVerbal Minddancer
Robert Gibbons
Neetu Wali
Shareef Abdur-Rasheed
Kimberly Burnham
William S. Peters, Sr.

Narcissus

December Feature Poets
Katherine Wyatt * WrittenInRed * Santosh Bakaya * Justin Pinke

Now Available

www.innerchildpress.com/the-year-of-the-poet

THE YEAR OF THE POET II
January 2015

Garnet

The Poetry Posse

Jamie Bond
Gail Weston Shazor
Albert 'Infinite' Carrasco
Siddartha Beth Pierce
Janet P. Caldwell
Tony Henninger
Joe DaVerbal Minddancer
Robert Gibbons
Neetu Wali
Shareef Abdur – Rasheed
Kimberly Burnham
Ann White
Keith Alan Hamilton
Katherine Wyatt
Fahredin Shehu
Hülya N. Yılmaz
Teresa E. Gallion
Jackie Allen
William S. Peters, Sr.

January Feature Poets

Bismay Mohanti * Jen Walls * Eric Judah

THE YEAR OF THE POET II
February 2015

Amethyst

THE POETRY POSSE

Jamie Bond
Gail Weston Shazor
Albert 'Infinite' Carrasco
Siddartha Beth Pierce
Janet P. Caldwell
Tony Henninger
Joe DaVerbal Minddancer
Robert Gibbons
Neetu Wali
Shareef Abdur – Rasheed
Kimberly Burnham
Ann White
Keith Alan Hamilton
Katherine Wyatt
Fahredin Shehu
Hülya N. Yılmaz
Teresa E. Gallion
Jackie Allen
William S. Peters, Sr.

FEBRUARY FEATURE POETS

Iram Fatima * Bob McNeil * Kerstin Centervall

The Year of the Poet II
March 2015

Our Featured Poets

Heung Sook * Anthony Arnold * Alicia Poland

Bloodstone

The Poetry Posse 2015

Jamie Bond * Gail Weston Shazor * Albert 'Infinite' Carrasco
Siddartha Beth Pierce * Janet P. Caldwell * Tony Henninger
Joe DaVerbal Minddancer * Neetu Wali * Shareef Abdur – Rasheed
Kimberly Burnham * Ann White * Keith Alan Hamilton
Katherine Wyatt * Fahredin Shehu * Hülya N. Yılmaz
Teresa E. Gallion * Jackie Allen * William S. Peters, Sr

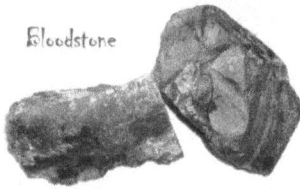

The Year of the Poet II
April 2015

Celebrating International Poetry Month

Our Featured Poets

Raja Williams * Dennis Ferado * Laure Charazac

Diamonds

The Poetry Posse 2015

Jamie Bond * Gail Weston Shazor * Albert 'Infinite' Carrasco
Siddartha Beth Pierce * Janet P. Caldwell * Tony Henninger
Joe DaVerbal Minddancer * Neetu Wali * Shareef Abdur – Rasheed
Kimberly Burnham * Ann White * Keith Alan Hamilton
Katherine Wyatt * Fahredin Shehu * Hülya N. Yılmaz
Teresa E. Gallion * Jackie Allen * William S. Peters, Sr.

Now Available

www.innerchildpress.com/the-year-of-the-poet

The Year of the Poet II
May 2015

May's Featured Poets
Geri Algeri
Akin Mosi Chinnery
Anna Jakubcza

Emeralds

The Poetry Posse 2015

Jamie Bond * Gail Weston Shazor * Albert 'Infinite' Carrasco
Siddartha Beth Pierce * Janet P. Caldwell * Tony Henninger
Joe DaVerbal Minddancer * Neetu Wali * Shareef Abdur – Rasheed
Kimberly Burnham * Ann White * Keith Alan Hamilton
Katherine Wyatt * Fahredin Shehu * Hülya N. Yılmaz
Teresa E. Gallion * Jackie Allen * William S. Peters, Sr.

The Year of the Poet II
June 2015

June's Featured Poets
Anahit Arustamyan * Yvette D. Murrell * Regina A. Walker

Pearl

The Poetry Posse 2015

Jamie Bond * Gail Weston Shazor * Albert 'Infinite' Carrasco
Siddartha Beth Pierce * Janet P. Caldwell * Tony Henninger
Joe DaVerbal Minddancer * Neetu Wali * Shareef Abdur – Rasheed
Kimberly Burnham * Ann White * Keith Alan Hamilton
Katherine Wyatt * Fahredin Shehu * Hülya N. Yılmaz
Teresa E. Gallion * Jackie Allen * William S. Peters, Sr

The Year of the Poet II
July 2015

The Featured Poets for July 2015
Abhik Shome * Christina Neal * Robert Neal

Rubies

The Poetry Posse 2015

Jamie Bond * Gail Weston Shazor * Albert 'Infinite' Carrasco
Siddartha Beth Pierce * Janet P. Caldwell * Tony Henninger
Joe DaVerbal Minddancer * Neetu Wali * Shareef Abdur – Rasheed
Kimberly Burnham * Ann White * Keith Alan Hamilton
Katherine Wyatt * Fahredin Shehu * Hülya N. Yılmaz
Teresa E. Gallion * Jackie Allen * William S. Peters, Sr.

The Year of the Poet II
August 2015

Peridot

Featured Poets
Gayle Howell
Ann Chalasz
Christopher Schultz

The Poetry Posse 2015

Jamie Bond * Gail Weston Shazor * Albert 'Infinite' Carrasco
Siddartha Beth Pierce * Janet P. Caldwell * Tony Henninger
Joe DaVerbal Minddancer * Neetu Wali * Shareef Abdur – Rasheed
Kimberly Burnham * Ann White * Keith Alan Hamilton
Katherine Wyatt * Fahredin Shehu * Hülya N. Yılmaz
Teresa E. Gallion * Jackie Allen * William S. Peters, Sr

Now Available

www.innerchildpress.com/the-year-of-the-poet

The Year of the Poet II

Featured Poets
Alfreda Ghee   Lonneice Weeks Badley   Demetrios Trifiatis

Sapphires

The Poetry Posse 2015

Jamie Bond * Gail Weston Shazor * Albert 'Infinite' Carrasco
Siddartha Beth Pierce * Janet P. Caldwell * Tony Henninger
Joe DaVerbal Minddancer * Neetu Wali * Shareef Abdur – Rasheed
Kimberly Burnham * Ann White * Keith Alan Hamilton
Katherine Wyatt * Fahredin Shehu * Hülya N. Yılmaz
Teresa E. Gallion * Jackie Allen * William S. Peters, Sr.

The Year of the Poet II
October 2015

Featured Poets
Monte Smith * Laura J. Wolfe * William Washington

Opal

The Poetry Posse 2015

Jamie Bond * Gail Weston Shazor * Albert 'Infinite' Carrasco
Siddartha Beth Pierce * Janet P. Caldwell * Tony Henninger
Joe DaVerbal Minddancer * Neetu Wali * Shareef Abdur – Rasheed
Kimberly Burnham * Ann White * Keith Alan Hamilton
Katherine Wyatt * Fahredin Shehu * Hülya N. Yılmaz
Teresa E. Gallion * Jackie Allen * William S. Peters, Sr.

The Year of the Poet II
November 2015

Featured Poets
Alan W. Jankowski
Bismay Mohanty
James Moore

Topaz

The Poetry Posse 2015

Jamie Bond * Gail Weston Shazor * Albert 'Infinite' Carrasco
Siddartha Beth Pierce * Janet P. Caldwell * Tony Henninger
Joe DaVerbal Minddancer * Neetu Wali * Shareef Abdur – Rasheed
Kimberly Burnham * Ann White * Keith Alan Hamilton
Katherine Wyatt * Fahredin Shehu * Hülya N. Yılmaz
Teresa E. Gallion * Jackie Allen * William S. Peters, Sr

The Year of the Poet II
December 2015

Featured Poets
Kerione Bryan * Michelle Joan Barulich * Neville Hiatt

Turquoise

The Poetry Posse 2015

Jamie Bond * Gail Weston Shazor * Albert 'Infinite' Carrasco
Siddartha Beth Pierce * Janet P. Caldwell * Tony Henninger
Joe DaVerbal Minddancer * Neetu Wali * Shareef Abdur – Rasheed
Kimberly Burnham * Ann White * Keith Alan Hamilton
Katherine Wyatt * Fahredin Shehu * Hülya N. Yılmaz
Teresa E. Gallion * Jackie Allen * William S. Peters, Sr.

Now Available

www.innerchildpress.com/the-year-of-the-poet

The Year of the Poet III — January 2016
Featured Poets
Lana Joseph * Atom Cyrus Rush * Christena Williams
Dark-eyed Junco
The Poetry Posse 2016

The Year of the Poet III — February 2016
Featured Poets
Anthony Arnold
Anna Chalasz
Andre Hawthorne
Puffin
The Poetry Posse 2016

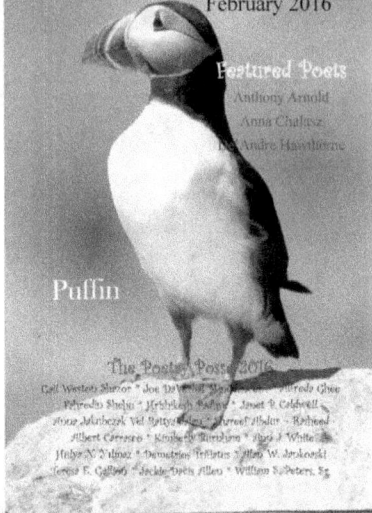

The Year of the Poet — March 2016
Featured Poets
Jeton Kelmendi   Nizar Sartawi   Sami Muhanna
Robin
The Poetry Posse 2016

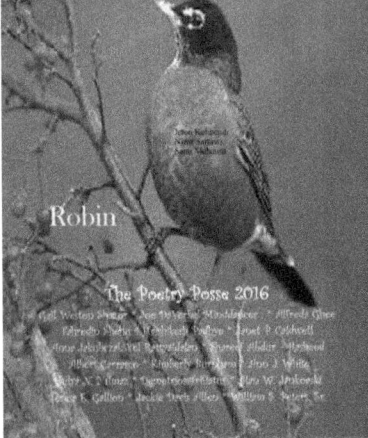

The Year of the Poet III
Featured Poets
Ali Abdolrezaei
Anna Chalasz
Agim Vinca
Ceri Naz
Black Capped Chickadee
The Poetry Posse 2016
celebrating international poetry month

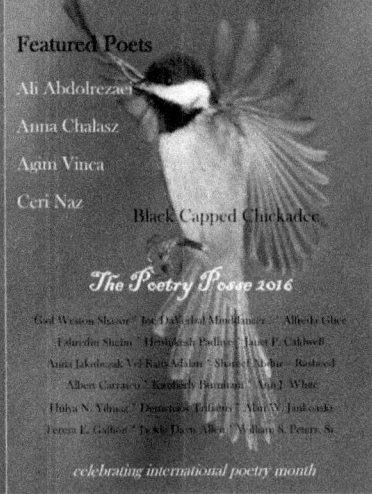

Now Available

www.innerchildpress.com/the-year-of-the-poet

The Year of the Poet
May 2016

Bob Strum
Barbara Allan
D.L. Davis

Oriole

The Year of the Poet III
June 2016

Featured Poets

Qibrije Demiri- Frangu
Naime Beqiraj
Faleeha Hassan
Bedri Zyberaj

Black Necked Stilt

The Poetry Posse 2016

The Year of the Poet III
July 2016

Iram Fatima 'Ashi'
Langley Shazor
Jody Doty
Emilia T. Davis

Indigo Bunting

The Poetry Posse 2016

The Year of the Poet III
August 2016

Featured Poets

Anita Dash
Irena Jovanovic
Malgorzata Gouluda

Painted Bunting

The Poetry Posse 2016

Now Available

www.innerchildpress.com/the-year-of-the-poet

The Year of the Poet III
September 2016

Featured Poets

Simone Weber
Abhijit Sen
Eunice Barbara C. Novio

Long Billed Curle

The Poetry Posse 2016

The Year of the Poet III
October 2016

Featured Poets

Lana Joseph
Sai Krishnamurthy
Jimes Moore

Barn Owl

The Poetry Posse 2016

The Year of the Poet III
November 2016

Featured Poets

Rosemary Burns
Robin Ouzman Hislop
Lonneice Weeks-Badley

Northern Cardinal

The Poetry Posse 2016

The Year of the Poet III
December 2016

Featured Poets

Samih Masoud
Mountassir Aziz Bien
Abdulkadir Musa

Rough Legged Hawk

The Poetry Posse 2016

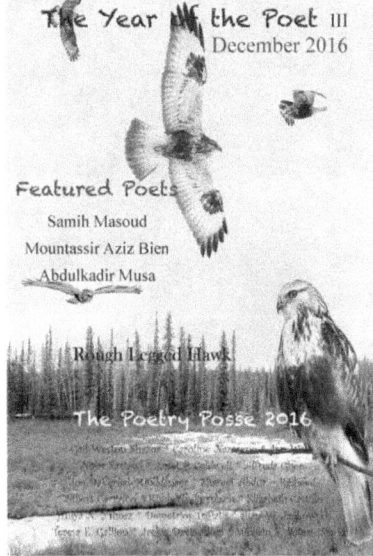

Now Available

www.innerchildpress.com/the-year-of-the-poet

The Year of the Poet IV
January 2017

Featured Poets
Jon Winell
Natalie Shields
Hanl Fatima Ashi

Quaking Aspen

The Poetry Posse 2017

Gail Weston Shazor * Caroline Nazareno * Shirley Mohanty
Nizar Sartawi * Anna Jakubczak Vel Ratty Adalan * Jen Walls
Joe DaVerbal Minddancer * Shareef Abdur - Rasheed
Albert Carrasco * Kimberly Burnham * Elizabeth Castillo
Hülya N. Yılmaz * Teleaha Hosam * Alan W. Jankowski
Teresa E. Gallion * Jackie Davis Allen * William S. Peters, Sr.

The Year of the Poet IV
February 2017

Featured Poets
Lin Ross
Soukaina Fathi
Onwer Gitani

Witch Hazel

The Poetry Posse 2017

Gail Weston Shazor * Caroline Nazareno * Shirley Mohanty
Nizar Sartawi * Anna Jakubczak Vel Ratty Adalan * Jen Walls
Joe DaVerbal Minddancer * Shareef Abdur - Rasheed
Albert Carrasco * Kimberly Burnham * Elizabeth Castillo
Hülya N. Yılmaz * Teleaha Hosam * Alan W. Jankowski
Teresa E. Gallion * Jackie Davis Allen * William S. Peters, Sr.

The Year of the Poet IV
March 2017

Featured Poets
Tremell Stevens
Francisca Ricinski
Jamil Abu Shaih

The Eastern Redbud

The Poetry Posse 2017

Gail Weston Shazor * Caroline Nazareno * Shirley Mohanty
Teresa E. Gallion * Anna Jakubczak Vel Ratty Adalan
Joe DaVerbal Minddancer * Shareef Abdur - Rasheed
Albert Carrasco * Kimberly Burnham * Elizabeth Castillo
Hülya N. Yılmaz * Teleaha Hosam * Jackie Davis Allen
Jen Walls * Nizar Sartawi * William S. Peters, Sr.

The Year of the Poet IV
April 2017

Featured Poets
Dr. Rachida Barmaki
Neptune Barman
Masood Khalaf

The Blossoming Cherry

The Poetry Posse 2017

Gail Weston Shazor * Caroline Nazareno * Shirley Mohanty
Teresa E. Gallion * Anna Jakubczak Vel Ratty Adalan
Joe DaVerbal Minddancer * Shareef Abdur - Rasheed
Albert Carrasco * Kimberly Burnham * Elizabeth Castillo
Hülya N. Yılmaz * Teleaha Hosam * Jackie Davis Allen
Jen Walls * Nizar Sartawi * William S. Peters, Sr.

Now Available

www.innerchildpress.com/the-year-of-the-poet

The Year of the Poet IV
May 2017

The Flowering Dogwood Tree

Featured Poets
Kallisa Powell
Alicja Maria Kuberska
Fethi Sassi

The Poetry Posse 2017

Gail Weston Shazor * Caroline Nazareno * Jhmmy Mohanty
Teresa E. Gallion * Anna Jakubczak Vel Ratty Adalan
Joe DeVerhol Straddmaer * Shareef Abdur - Rasheed
Albert Carrasco * Kimberly Burnham * Elizabeth Castillo
Hülya N. Yılmaz * Falesha Hasan * Jackie Davis Allen
Jen Walls * Nizar Sartawi * * William S. Peters, Sr.

The Year of the Poet IV
June 2017

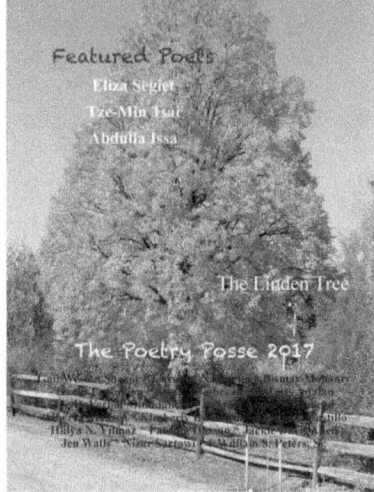

Featured Poets
Eliza Segiet
Tze-Min Tsai
Abdulla Issa

The Linden Tree

The Poetry Posse 2017

Hülya N. Yılmaz * Falesha Hasan * Jackie Davis Allen
Jen Walls * Nizar Sartawi * * William S. Peters, Sr.

The Year of the Poet IV
July 2017

Featured Poets
Anca Mihaela Bruma
Ibaa Ismail
Zvonko Taneski

The Oak Moon

The Poetry Posse 2017

The Year of the Poet IV
August 2017

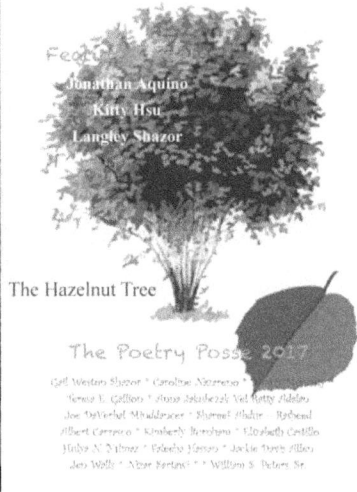

Featured Poets
Jonathan Aquino
Kitty Hsu
Langley Shazor

The Hazelnut Tree

The Poetry Posse 2017

Gail Weston Shazor * Caroline Nazareno *
Teresa E. Gallion * Anna Jakubczak Vel Ratty Adalan
Joe DeVerhol Straddmaer * Shareef Abdur - Rasheed
Albert Carrasco * Kimberly Burnham * Elizabeth Castillo
Hülya N. Yılmaz * Falesha Hasan * Jackie Davis Allen
Jen Walls * Nizar Sartawi * * William S. Peters, Sr.

Now Available

www.innerchildpress.com/the-year-of-the-poet

The Year of the Poet IV
September 2017

Featured Poets
Martina Reisz Newberry
Ameer Nassir
Christine Fulco Neal
Robert Neal

The Elm Tree

The Poetry Posse 2017

Gail Weston Shazor * Caroline Nazareno * Bismay Mohanty
Teresa E. Gallion * Anna Jakubczak Vel Ratty Adalan
Joe DaVerbal Minddancer * Shareef Abdur – Rasheed
Albert Carrasco * Kimberly Burnham * Elizabeth Castillo
Hülya N. Yılmaz * Faleeha Hassan * Jackie Davis Allen
Jen Walls * Nizar Sartawi * * William S. Peters, Sr.

The Year of the Poet IV
October 2017

Featured Poets
Ahmed Abu Saleem
Nedal Al-Qaeim
Sadeddin Shalon

The Black Walnut Tree

The Poetry Posse 2017

Gail Weston Shazor * Caroline Nazareno * Bismay Mohanty
Teresa E. Gallion * Anna Jakubczak Vel Ratty Adalan
Joe DaVerbal Minddancer * Shareef Abdur – Rasheed
Albert Carrasco * Kimberly Burnham * Elizabeth Castillo
Hülya N. Yılmaz * Faleeha Hassan * Jackie Davis Allen
Jen Walls * Nizar Sartawi * * William S. Peters, Sr.

The Year of the Poet IV
November 2017

Featured Poets
Kay Peters
Alfreda D. Ghee
Gabriella Garofalo
Rosemary Cappello

The Tree of Life

The Poetry Posse 2017

Gail Weston Shazor * Caroline Nazareno * Bismay Mohanty
Teresa E. Gallion * Anna Jakubczak Vel Ratty Adalan
Joe DaVerbal Minddancer * Shareef Abdur – Rasheed
Albert Carrasco * Kimberly Burnham * Elizabeth Castillo
Hülya N. Yılmaz * Faleeha Hassan * Jackie Davis Allen
Jen Walls * Nizar Sartawi * William S. Peters, Sr.

The Year of the Poet IV
December 2017

Featured Poets
Justice Clarke
Mariel M. Pabroa
Kiley Brown

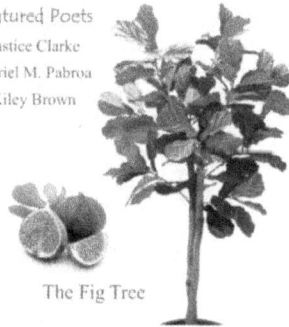

The Fig Tree

The Poetry Posse 2017

Gail Weston Shazor * Caroline Nazareno * Bismay Mohanty
Teresa E. Gallion * Anna Jakubczak Vel Ratty Adalan
Joe DaVerbal Minddancer * Shareef Abdur – Rasheed
Albert Carrasco * Kimberly Burnham * Elizabeth Castillo
Hülya N. Yılmaz * Faleeha Hassan * Jackie Davis Allen
Jen Walls * Nizar Sartawi * William S. Peters, Sr.

Now Available

www.innerchildpress.com/the-year-of-the-poet

The Year of the Poet V
January 2018
Featured Poets
Iyad Shamasnah
Yasmeen Hamzeh
Ali Abdolrezaei

Aksum

The Poetry Posse 2018
Gail Weston Shazor * Caroline Nazareno * Tezmin Ition Tsai
Hülya N. Yılmaz * Faleeha Hassan * Jackie Davis Allen
Teresa E. Gallion * Anna Jakubczak Vel Ratty Adalan
Alicja Maria Kuberska * Shareef Abdur ~ Rasheed
Kimberly Burnham * Elizabeth Castillo
Nizar Sartawi * William S. Peters, Sr.

The Year of the Poet V
February 2018

Sabean

Featured Poets
Muhammad Azram
Anna Szawrnicka
Abhilipsa Kuanar
Aanika Aery

The Poetry Posse 2018
Gail Weston Shazor * Caroline Nazareno * Tezmin Ition Tsai
Hülya N. Yılmaz * Faleeha Hassan * Jackie Davis Allen
Teresa E. Gallion * Anna Jakubczak Vel Ratty Adalan
Alicja Maria Kuberska * Shareef Abdur ~ Rasheed
Kimberly Burnham * Elizabeth Castillo
Nizar Sartawi * William S. Peters, Sr.

The Year of the Poet V
March 2018

Featured Poets
Iram Fatima 'Ashi'
Cassandra Swan
Jaleel Khazaal
Shazni Zaman

Mexico   Cuba
Belize   Dominican
Guatemala   Jamaica Republic
  El Salvador Nicaragua Haiti Puerto Rico
Caribbean   Costa Rica Panama
&   Colombia
Middle America

The Poetry Posse 2018
Gail Weston Shazor * Nizar Sartawi * Hülya N. Yılmaz
Jackie Davis Allen * Caroline 'Ceri' Nazareno
Alicja Maria Kuberska * Teresa E. Gallion
Faleeha Hassan * Shareef Abdur ~ Rasheed
Kimberly Burnham * Elizabeth Castillo
Tezmin Ition Tsai * William S. Peters, Sr.

The Year of the Poet V
April 2018

Featured Poets

The Nez Perce

The Poetry Posse 2018

Now Available

www.innerchildpress.com/the-year-of-the-poet

168

The Year of the Poet V
May 2018

Featured Poets
Zaldy Carreci de Leon Jr.
Sylvia K. Malinowska
Loukía Abreu
Otilia Prodan

The Sumerians

The Poetry Posse 2018
Gail Weston Shazor * Nizar Sartawi * Hülya N. Yılmaz
Jackie Davis Allen * Caroline 'Ceri' Nazareno
Alicja Maria Kuberska * Teresa E. Gallion
Kimberly Burnham * Shareef Abdur – Rasheed
Faleeha Hassan * Elizabeth Castillo * Swapna Behera
Tezmin Ition Tsai * William S. Peters, Sr.

The Year of the Poet V
June 2018

Featured Poets
Bilall Maliqi * Daim Miftari * Gojko Božović * Sofija Živkova

The Paleo Indians

The Poetry Posse 2018

The Year of the Poet V
July 2018

Oceania

The Poetry Posse 2018

The Year of the Poet V
August 2018

Featured Poets
Hussein Habasch * Mircea Dan Duta * Naida Mujkić * Swagat Das

The Lapita

The Poetry Posse 2018
Gail Weston Shazor * Nizar Sartawi * Hülya N. Yılmaz
Jackie Davis Allen * Caroline 'Ceri' Nazareno
Alicja Maria Kuberska * Teresa E. Gallion
Kimberly Burnham * Shareef Abdur – Rasheed
Ashok K. Bhargava * Elizabeth Castillo * Swapna Behera
Tezmin Ition Tsai * William S. Peters, Sr.

Now Available

www.innerchildpress.com/the-year-of-the-poet

The Year of the Poet V
September 2018

The Aztecs & Incas

Featured Poets
Kolade Olanrewaju Freedom
Elijah Sequoi
Mazher Hussain Abdul Ghani
Lily Swarn

The Poetry Posse 2018

Gail Weston Shazor * Nizar Sartawi * Hülya N. Yılmaz
Jackie Davis Allen * Caroline 'Ceri' Nazareno
Alicja Maria Kubenska * Teresa E. Gallion
Kimberly Burnham * Shareef Abdur - Rasheed
Ashok K. Bhargava * Elizabeth Castillo * Swapna Behera
Teznim Htoo Tsu * William S. Peters, Sr.

The Year of the Poet V
October 2018

Featured Poets
Alicia Minjarez * Lonnelee Weeks-Badley
Lopamudra Mishra * Abdelwahed Souayah

Bengali

The Poetry Posse 2018

Gail Weston Shazor * Nizar Sartawi * Hülya N. Yılmaz
Jackie Davis Allen * Caroline 'Ceri' Nazareno
Alicja Maria Kubenska * Teresa E. Gallion
Kimberly Burnham * Shareef Abdur – Rasheed
Ashok K. Bhargava * Elizabeth Castillo * Swapna Behera
Teznin Htoo Tsu * William S. Peters, Sr.

Now Available

www.innerchildpress.com/the-year-of-the-poet

and there is much, much more !

visit . . .

http://www.innerchildpress.com
/anthologies-sales-special.php

Also check out our Authors and
all the wonderful Books
Available at :

http://www.innerchildpress.com
/the-book-store.php

WORLD HEALING
WORLD PEACE
2018

INNER CHILD PRESS

A Poetry Anthology for Humanity

Now Available

www.worldhealingworldpeacepoetry.com

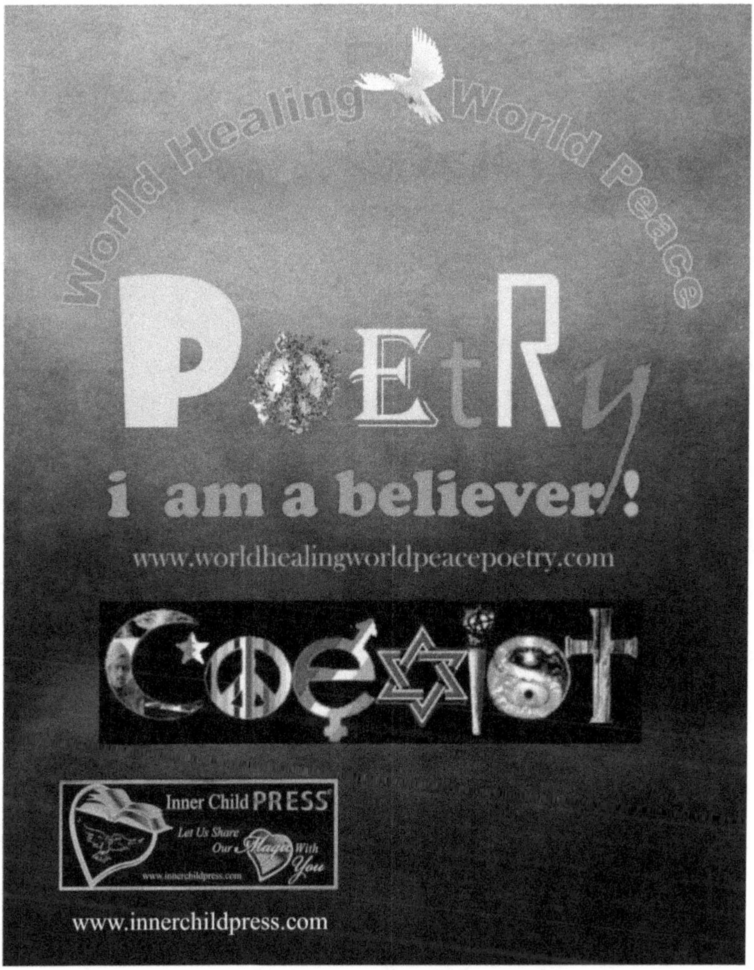

Now Available

www.worldhealingworldpeacepoetry.com

World Healing
World Peace

support

www.worldhealingworldpeacepoetry.com

174

World Healing
World Peace
2018

Now Available

www.worldhealingworldpeacepoetry.com

nner Child Press International

'building cultural bridges of understanding'

Meet our Cultural Ambassadors

Fahredin Shehu
Director of Cultural
International

Faleha Hassan
Iraq ~ USA

Elizabeth E. Castillo
Philippines

Kimberly Burnham
Pacific Northwest
USA

Alicja Kuberska
Poland
Eastern Europe

Swapna Behera
India
Southeast Asia

Ashok K. Bhargava
Canada

Tzemin Ition Tsai
Republic of China
Greater China

Laure Charazac
France
Western Europe

www.innerchildpress.com

This Anthological Publication
is underwritten solely by

Inner Child Press

Inner Child Press is a Publishing Company
Founded and Operated by Writers. Our personal
publishing experiences provides us an intimate
understanding of the sometimes daunting
challenges Writers, New and Seasoned may face in
the Business of Publishing and Marketing their
Creative "Written Work".

For more Information

Inner Child Press

www.innerchildpress.com

~ fini ~